THE RIGHT TO BEAR ARMS

Other books in this series:

The Bill of Rights

THE RIGHT TO BEAR ARMS

Edited by Robert Winters

Bruce Glassman, *Vice President*
Bonnie Szumski, *Publisher*
Helen Cothran, *Managing Editor*
Scott Barbour, *Series Editor*

GREENHAVEN PRESS
A part of Gale, Cengage Learning

Detroit • New York • San Francisco • New Haven, Conn • Waterville, Maine • London

GALE
CENGAGE Learning·

LIBRARY OF CONGRESS CATALOGING-IN-PUBLICATION DATA

The right to bear arms / Robert Winters, book editor.
   p. cm. — (The bill of rights)
  Includes bibliographical references and index.
  ISBN 0-7377-1933-8 (lib. : alk. paper)
  1. Firearms—Law and legislation—United States. 2. Gun control—United States. I. Winters, Robert, 1963– . II. Bill of Rights (San Diego, Calif.)
  KF3941.R54 2006
  344.73'0533—dc22

                              2005046386

Printed in the United States of America
5 6 7 13 12 11 10 09

"I cannot agree with those who think of the Bill of Rights as an 18th Century straightjacket, unsuited for this age. . . . The evils it guards against are not only old, they are with us now, they exist today."

—Hugo Black, associate justice of the
U.S. Supreme Court, 1937–1971

The Bill of Rights codifies the freedoms most essential to American democracy. Freedom of speech, freedom of religion, the right to bear arms, the right to a trial by a jury of one's peers, the right to be free from cruel and unusual punishment—these are just a few of the liberties that the Founding Fathers thought it necessary to spell out in the first ten amendments to the U.S. Constitution.

While the document itself is quite short (consisting of fewer than five hundred words), and while the liberties it protects often seem straightforward, the Bill of Rights has been a source of debate ever since its creation. Throughout American history, the rights the document protects have been tested and reinterpreted. Again and again, individuals perceiving violations of their rights have sought redress in the courts. The courts in turn have struggled to decipher the original intent of the founders as well as the need to accommodate changing societal norms and values.

The ultimate responsibility for addressing these claims has fallen to the U.S. Supreme Court. As the highest court in the nation, it is the Supreme Court's role to interpret the Constitution. The Court has considered numerous cases in which people have accused government of impinging on their rights. In the process, the Court has established a body of case law and precedents that have, in a sense, defined the Bill of Rights. In doing so, the Court has often reversed itself and introduced new ideas and approaches that have altered the legal meaning of the rights contained in the Bill of Rights. As a general rule, the Court has erred on the side of caution, upholding and expanding the rights of individuals rather than restricting them.

An example of this trend is the definition of cruel and unusual punishment. The Eighth Amendment specifically states, "Excessive bail shall not be required, nor excessive fines imposed, nor cruel and unusual punishments inflicted." However, over the years the Court has had to grapple with defining what constitutes "cruel and unusual punishment." In colonial America, punishments for crimes included branding, the lopping off of ears, and whipping. Indeed, these punishments were considered lawful at the time the Bill of Rights was written. Obviously, none of these punishments are legal today. In order to justify outlawing certain types of punishment that are deemed repugnant by the majority of citizens, the Court has ruled that it must consider the prevailing opinion of the masses when making such decisions. In overturning the punishment of a man stripped of his citizenship, the Court stated in 1958 that it must rely on society's "evolving standards of decency" when determining what constitutes cruel and unusual punishment. Thus the definition of cruel and unusual is not frozen to include only the types of punishment that were illegal at the time of the framing of the Bill of Rights; specific modes of punishment can be rejected as society deems them unjust.

Another way that the Courts have interpreted the Bill of Rights to expand individual liberties is through the process of "incorporation." Prior to the passage of the Fourteenth Amendment, the Bill of Rights was thought to prevent only the federal government from infringing on the rights listed in the document. However, the Fourteenth Amendment, which was passed in the wake of the Civil War, includes the words, ". . . nor shall any state deprive any person of life, liberty, or property, without due process of law; nor deny to any person within its jurisdiction the equal protection of the laws." Citing this passage, the Court has ruled that many of the liberties contained in the Bill of Rights apply to state and local governments as well as the federal government. This process of incorporation laid the legal foundation for the civil rights movement—most specifically the 1954 *Brown v. Board of Education* ruling that put an end to legalized segregation.

As these examples reveal, the Bill of Rights is not static. It truly is a living document that is constantly being reinterpreted and redefined. The Bill of Rights series captures this vital aspect of one of America's most cherished founding texts. Each volume in the series focuses on one particular right protected in the Bill of Rights. Through the use of primary and secondary sources, the right's evolution is traced from colonial times to the present. Primary sources include landmark Supreme Court rulings, speeches by prominent experts, and editorials. Secondary sources include historical analyses, law journal articles, book excerpts, and magazine articles. Each book also includes several features to facilitate research, including a bibliography, an annotated table of contents, an annotated list of relevant Supreme Court cases, an introduction, and an index. These elements help to make the Bill of Rights series a fascinating and useful tool for examining the fundamental liberties of American democracy.

The Second Amendment to the U.S. Constitution contains two clauses: "A well regulated Militia being necessary to the security of a free State, the right of the people to keep and bear Arms shall not be infringed." The meaning of these two phrases, both separately and together, is the source of voluminous debate. Indeed, perhaps no other passage of the Bill of Rights is subject to as much scrutiny and interpretation as these twenty-seven words. Advocates of gun control tend to focus on the first clause. They argue that the amendment is intended to protect a collective right of states to maintain armed militias for defense against foreign invasions or a tyrannical federal government. Proponents of greater gun rights on the other hand, emphasize the second clause. They insist that the amendment's purpose is to protect the rights of individuals to possess weapons for their personal use. Although this use may include participation in a militia, it need not be limited to such use. Historians, legal scholars, and commentators on every side struggle to reconcile these two views and to define an amendment that seems to be at odds with itself.

This question about the meaning of the Second Amendment is more than a linguistic debate. The answer determines whether gun control laws are constitutional. If the right to own guns is purely individual—like the right to free speech or the freedom of religion—the government has no business stepping in and limiting it to certain groups or for certain purposes. If it is a collective right, designed to protect the states from federal encroachments or foreign invasions, then government has every right, and indeed an obligation, to decide what regulations are necessary. The nature of the issue, literally a matter of life and death, probably makes controversy inevitable, but Supreme Court decisions have done little to bring about a final resolution of the debate.

The Supreme Court Allows Some Regulations

The Court's decisions on gun control have tended to be quite specific, and both sides find support for their positions in the Court's rulings. However, the overall trend has been to give Congress, as well as state governments, a great deal of leeway in regulating guns while indicating that an outright ban on gun ownership would be unconstitutional.

Two cases from the late 1800s give an indication of the Court's position. *U.S. v. Cruikshank,* decided in 1875, involved the conviction of a group of white supremacists who had burned down a courthouse and killed over one hundred black men trying to defend their rights in post–Civil War Louisiana. Cruikshank and the other ringleaders of the attack were convicted of violating the civil rights of the assembled black men. Significantly, they were convicted in a federal rather than state court, based on the belief that they had deprived their victims of certain federal rights, including their Second Amendment right to bear arms. An appeals court set the defendants free, and the Supreme Court agreed with that decision in a conclusion that still causes confusion and heated argument.

The Court held that the Second Amendment limited the powers of the federal government, not state governments or individuals. In this case it was individuals who had allegedly violated the victims' rights, so in the Court's view the Second Amendment did not apply. However, the ruling also referred to the right to bear arms, among other rights, as predating the Constitution and not necesarily dependent on it. Thus the Court indicated that the Second Amendment did not forbid state governments from passing gun control laws, but it also upheld an individual right to gun ownership.

In *Presser v. Illinois,* decided in 1886, the Court was confronted with a more clear-cut case of governmental power. Here, the state of Illinois prosecuted a German immigrant named Herman Presser, who had formed his own private militia to protect the rights of working-class Germans. When the militia held a parade, carrying rifles, the state of Illinois arrested Presser for maintaining a private militia. Presser, in turn, maintained that his arrest violated his right to as-

sembly and his right to bear arms. This time the Court upheld the conviction, finding that the state had a right to establish its own militia and prevent private citizens from
forming their own. Again, the Court ruled that the Second
Amendment was really a federal matter, limiting the actions
of Congress rather than state legislatures. At the same time,
the Court held that the national government has a constitutional interest in state militias as a bulwark of national defense; therefore, the states could not go so far as to actually
disarm their citizens or otherwise eliminate their effectiveness as militia members.

The precedent set by *Cruikshank* and *Presser*—that the
Second Amendment limits the federal government rather
than state governments—still stands today. In this regard
the right to bear arms differs from most rights listed in the
Bill of Rights. During the middle and late twentieth century,
the Supreme Court began to interpret the Bill of Rights in
light of the Fourteenth Amendment. That amendment,
passed in the wake of the Civil War, contains clauses that
forbid states from violating the rights of citizens. In a process
known as "selective incorporation," the Court in a series of
rulings has declared that the vast majority of rights codified
in the Bill of Rights are protected against state as well as
federal violation. The right to bear arms is one of only a few
rights that have never been incorporated.

The *Miller* Decision

In *U.S. v. Miller*, the Court was confronted with a federal law,
and thus the issue had nothing to do with incorporation or
states' rights. Instead, the Court was asked to rule on a case
involving the National Firearms Act of 1934, which mandated registration of various weapons, including shotguns
less than eighteen inches in length. Jack Miller and Frank
Layton had been convicted of transporting an unregistered
sawed-off shotgun over state lines. On appeal, the conviction
was overturned by the District Court of the Western District
of Arkansas, which argued that the National Firearms Act
was itself unconstitutional in mandating this registration.
The Department of Justice appealed to the Supreme Court.

In reinstating Miller's original conviction, the Court went beyond upholding the constitutionality of the National Firearms Act. It also stated that possession of a particular weapon had to have "some reasonable relationship to the preservation or efficiency of a well regulated militia" in order to be protected by the Second Amendment. This 1939 ruling still provides the primary justification for federal gun control. However, while the Court has clearly upheld some regulatory role for the federal government, it also made clear that the government can never go so far as to threaten an underlying purpose of the Second Amendment: preserving the state militias.

Gun rights advocates focus on this support for state militias in *Miller* because they insist it confirms their view that the Second Amendment protects an individual right to gun ownership. Although the ruling upheld gun rights in the context of militias, the Court acknowledged that at the time of the nation's founding, militias included the vast majority of able-bodied males. For example, it noted that militias included "civilians primarily, soldiers on occasion." In addition, it stated that when called up, militia members "were expected to appear bearing arms supplied by themselves and of the kind in common use at the time." This clearly implies that individual citizens, as potential militia members, have a constitutional right to possess certain weapons. Nevertheless, despite its support for gun ownership, *Miller* stands as a landmark decision providing the government with substantive leeway in regulating firearms for its own purposes, and since then the Court has clearly upheld that precedent.

The Supreme Court has repeatedly upheld government's regulatory power over guns, as demonstrated by its rulings in support of the federal Gun Control Act of 1968 and the 1994 Brady Handgun Violence Prevention Act. In 1980, in *Lewis v. United States,* the Court upheld a federal law banning convicted felons from gun ownership, stating in a footnote that "legislative restrictions on the use of firearms do not trench upon any constitutionally protected liberties." Taking their cue from these decisions, lower federal and state courts have likewise repeatedly upheld gun control legislation.

An Ongoing Debate

The Second Amendment and its interpretation remains a profoundly controversial and politically charged issue. The National Rifle Association boasts over 4 million members and provides hundreds of thousands of dollars in contributions to congressional campaigns. The clout of firearms owners and gun rights supporters is legendary in Washington and many state capitals. At the same time, according to a 2004 poll, approximately 60 percent of Americans support stricter gun control, and only 38 percent claimed to have a gun themselves. Organizations like Handgun Control, Inc. and the Million Mom March, and spokespeople such as Sarah Brady, whose husband was severely brain damaged during the assassination attempt on Ronald Reagan, have convinced Congress to enact background checks, trigger locks, and, at least temporarily, an outright ban on the sale of assault weapons (though Congress allowed this ban to lapse in September 2004).

The political climate is volatile and argumentative on this issue, and it seems clear that the Supreme Court will not step in to end this debate. Instead, it has made clear that the Second Amendment does not prevent Congress, much less the states, from regulating the right to gun ownership. At the same time, it has acknowledged some fundamental right to private ownership of guns as a support to state militias. In a 1789 letter to a colleague, Albert Gallatin, an important proponent of the new Constitution who later became Thomas Jefferson's secretary of the treasury, noted that "the whole of that Bill [of Rights] is a declaration of the right of the people at large or considered as individuals." The history of the Second Amendment seems designed as a sort of test case for determining whether "at large" or "as individuals" is the key phrase. Thus far, the Supreme Court's answer seems to be "yes, both."

CHAPTER ONE

The Founders' Intent in Creating the Second Amendment

The Bill of Rights

The Founders Intended to Protect Individual Gun Rights

Joyce Lee Malcolm

In recent years a number of historians and legal scholars have developed what is now called the "standard model" of interpreting the Second Amendment. According to this model, the founders clearly meant to ensure the individual's right to bear arms, just as the rest of the Bill of Rights guarantees individual rights. Joyce Lee Malcolm, a history professor at Bentley College and an expert in seventeenth-century England, is a prominent member of this school of interpretation. She traces the origins of this right to medieval England, where prominent subjects were required to keep arms in order to maintain public order and repel foreign invasion. Throughout the struggles of the seventeenth century, which culminated in the English Civil War and the execution of King Charles I, this obligation became a cherished right as a protection against tyranny. The American colonists inherited this tradition of individual gun rights and, like their medieval predecessors, colonial governments often required citizens to maintain arms for protection of themselves and their communities. Given this history, Malcolm believes that the founders had a strong attachment to an individual right of gun ownership. In the following excerpt she emphasizes that in passing the Second Amendment, the members of the First Congress clearly meant to preserve the individual's right to bear arms for self-protection and for national defense.

A lthough the Constitution had been ratified by the required nine states without amendment, this was accomplished with the promise that the new Congress would add amendments to protect liberties and restrict federal powers.

Joyce Lee Malcolm, *To Keep and Bear Arms: The Origins of an Anglo American Right.* Cambridge, MA: Harvard University Press, 1994. Copyright © 1994 by the President and Fellows of Harvard College. All rights reserved. Reproduced by permission.

When the first Congress of the United States convened on March 4, 1789, many congressmen believed that consideration of a bill of rights could be safely postponed, perhaps until their second session. Ironically, James Madison, who had advocated passage of the Constitution without such amendments, now pressed his colleagues to act. When his remarks failed to produce any response, Madison drafted his own version of a bill of rights and interrupted his colleagues on June 8 to present it to them. He explained to [Thomas] Jefferson several days later that he had selected those rights for inclusion which were unexceptional and thus most likely to win approval. He deliberately proposed amendments that would not detract from federal powers, among them a right for the citizenry to be armed. His version of what would eventually become the Second Amendment stated: "The right of the people to keep and bear arms shall not be infringed; a well armed, and well regulated militia being the best security of a free country: but no person religiously scrupulous of bearing arms, shall be compelled to render military service in person." He assumed that amendments protecting civil liberties would be most naturally accommodated within the body of the Constitution in the article which delineated the powers of Congress, section nine between the third and fourth clauses. The third clause forbade Congress from passing bills of attainder or *ex post facto* laws, the fourth referred to direct taxation.

It was another six weeks before Madison's amendments were discussed. The matter was then referred to a committee of three—Madison, John Vining of Delaware, and Roger Sherman of Connecticut. The committee was also to consider the numerous state proposals [recommendations for amendments submitted by state ratification conventions] and report back to the House.

Sherman's Suggestions

Nearly 200 years later, in 1987, a hitherto unknown draft for a bill of rights that Sherman apparently drew up for the consideration of the committee was found. While Sherman's suggested list differs in many respects from the committee's final report, it is extremely interesting both for Sherman's suggestions and for the changes his colleagues made. Sherman does not specifically mention an individual right to keep and bear arms, although this may have been implied in his second article, which referred to "certain natural rights" retained by the people, among which he listed that of "pursuing . . . Safety." [English judicial scholar William] Blackstone had referred to the right of Englishmen to have weapons as a "natural right of resistance and self preservation." The fifth of Sherman's eleven articles dealt with the militia but did not characterize it as "the best security" of a free country, or hint that it was preferable to a standing army. This article seems to have been intended to enhance somewhat the states' control of their militia. Sherman proposed that when not in the service of the United States, the militia be subject to state law, albeit their organization and discipline remain under federal jurisdiction. His proposal read: "The militia shall be under the government of the laws of the respective States, when not in the actual Service of the united States, but such rules as may be prescribed by Congress for their uniform organization and discipline shall be observed in officering and training them, but military Service shall not be required of persons religiously scrupulous of bearing arms."

The committee clearly found Sherman's omission of a stated right to have weapons and his attempt to enhance state authority unsatisfactory. Its own arms amendment remained close to Madison's language. It failed to mention state powers over the militia but proclaimed and protected "the right of the people" to have weapons. The committee agreed upon the following amendment: "A well regulated militia, composed of the body of the people, being the best security of a free state, the right of the people to keep and bear arms shall not be infringed; but no person religiously scrupulous shall be compelled to bear arms." The committee had amended Madison's article in several respects. In keeping with state proposals, the word "state" had been substituted for Madison's "country." "State" was a more precise term and, since a state was a polity, it could refer either to one state or to the United States. The language had also been tightened by reversing the reference to the militia and the right of the people to bear arms, perhaps intentionally putting more emphasis on the militia. Significantly, Madison's stipulation that the militia be well armed was omitted, but the committee added its own description of the militia as composed of the body of the people.

Senate Changes

There were further delays before the House considered the committee report. When it did so, it agreed to Sherman's proposal that amendments be added at the end of the Constitution rather than imbedded within it. This has long been regarded as Sherman's major contribution. The amendments were approved and forwarded to the Senate, where senators "slashed out wordiness with a free hand" [in the words of historian Robert Allen Rutland]. The third and fourth articles on the House list, for instance, were combined into the present First Amendment. The article on the right to have arms was altered, tightened, and abbreviated to its modern form: "A well regulated Militia being necessary to the security of a free State, the right of the people to keep and bear Arms, shall not be infringed." The militia was now described not as "the best security" of a free state but as "necessary to the security" of a free state, an even stronger endorsement than Madison's original description. The phrase describing the militia as "composed of the body of the people" was dropped. Elbridge Gerry's fear that future Congresses might expand the religious exemption from militia service to include everyone seems to have convinced the Senate to drop that clause as well.

Of even greater importance for an accurate understanding of the Senate's intentions are a suggested amendment and two proposals that the senators rejected. They turned down the recommendation of five states that standing armies in time of peace require explicit consent, and they denied a proposal to return to the states more power over their militia. And like the Convention Parliament in 1689,[1] the senators rejected a motion to add "for the common defense" after "to keep and bear

_____

[1] ~~ntion Parliament of 1689 was the first to meet after the Glorious 1688 deposed King James II in favor of King William III. The assed "An Act Declaring the Rights and Liberties of the Subject the Succession of the Crown," known more familiarly as the of Rights.

arms." The American Bill of Rights, like the English Bill of Rights, recognized the individual's right to have weapons for his own defence, rather than for collective defence. These decisions taken together make the task of deciphering the framers' intentions much surer. In this form, along with eleven other amendments, the Second Amendment was approved by Congress and sent to the state legislatures for ratification.

Misinterpretations of the Amendment

At each stage of its passage through Congress the arms amendment became less explicit. Doubtless congressmen felt no qualms about streamlining the language and omitting explanatory phrases because their constituents shared an understanding of the institutions and opinions behind it. But, in the long term, these understandings have vanished and brevity and elegance have been achieved at the cost of clarity. Modern writers, lacking the benefit of the historical tradition upon which the Second Amendment was based, have derived an astonishing variety of meanings from its single sentence. They argue, for example, that the purpose was only to preserve the states' powers over state militia; that the amendment merely protects the right of members of a militia—the National Guard of today—to be armed; and that the language "the right of the people to keep and bear arms" should not be interpreted to grant to any individual a right to own a weapon. Lawrence Cress, for example, has maintained that the term "the people" in the Second Amendment means that a "collective" rather than an individual right is intended. Yet this idiosyncratic definition founders because it cannot be reasonably applied to the First, Fourth, Ninth, and Tenth Amendments, where reference is also made to the right of "the people." The Second Amendment was the product of Anglo-American attitudes, prejudices, and policies toward standing armies, militia, citizenship, and personal rights. . . . This history can enable us to recapture and clarify the intention of the framers.

Goals of the Second Amendment

The Second Amendment was meant to accomplish two distinct goals, each perceived as crucial to the maintenance of liberty. First, it was meant to guarantee the individual's right to have arms for self-defence and self-preservation. Such an individual right was a legacy of the [1689] English Bill of Rights. This is also plain from American colonial practice, the debates over the Constitution, and state proposals for what was to become the Second Amendment. In keeping with colonial precedent, the American article broadened the English protection. English restrictions had limited the right to have arms to Protestants and made the type and quantity of such weapons dependent upon what was deemed "suitable" to a person's "condition." The English also included the proviso that the right to have arms was to be "as allowed by law." Americans swept aside these limitations and forbade any "infringement" upon the right of the people to keep and bear arms.

These privately owned arms were meant to serve a larger purpose as well, albeit the American framers of the Second Amendment, like their English predecessors, rejected language linking their right to "the common defence." When, as Blackstone phrased it, "the sanctions of society and laws are found insufficient to restrain the violence of oppression," these private weapons would afford the people the means to vindicate their liberties.

The second and related objective concerned the militia, and it is the coupling of these two objectives that has caused the most confusion. The customary American militia necessitated an armed public, and Madison's original version of the amendment, as well as those suggested by the states, described the militia as either "composed of" or "including" the body of the people. A select militia was regarded as little better than a standing army. The argument that today's National Guardsmen, members of a select militia, would constitute the *only* persons entitled to keep and bear arms has no historical foundation. Indeed, it would seem redundant to specify that members of a militia had the right to be armed. A militia could scarcely function otherwise. But the argument that this constitutional right to have weapons was exclusively for members of a militia falters on another ground. The House committee eliminated the stipulation that the militia be "well-armed," and the Senate, in what became the final version of the amendment, eliminated the description of the militia as composed of the "body of the people." These changes left open the possibility of a poorly armed and narrowly based militia that many Americans feared might be the result of federal control. Yet the amendment guaranteed that the right of "the people" to have arms not be infringed. Whatever the future composition of the militia, therefore, however well or ill armed, was not crucial because the people's right to have weapons was to be sacrosanct. As was the case in the English tradition, the arms in the hands of the people, not the militia, are relied upon "to restrain the violence of oppression."

Control of the Militia

The Constitution gave to the federal government broad authority over state militia. Was the Second Amendment meant to placate states fearful about this loss of control? In fact not one of the ninety-seven distinct amendments proposed by state ratifying conventions asked for a *return* of any control that had been allocated to the federal government over the militia. Sherman's proposal that some power be returned to the states was rejected by the drafting committee. In any event, the Second Amendment does nothing to alter the situation. Indeed, that was precisely the complaint of the anti-Federalist *Centinel* in a discussion of the House version of the arms article. The *Centinel* found that "the absolute command vested by other sections in Congress over the militia, are [sic] not in the least abridged by this amendment." Had the intent been to reapportion this power some diminution of federal control would have been mandated. None was.

The clause concerning the militia was not intended to limit ownership of arms to militia members, or return control of the militia to the states, but rather to express the preference for a militia over a standing army. The army had been written into the Constitution. Despite checks within the Constitution to make it responsive to civil authority, the army was considered a threat to liberty. State constitutions that

had a bill of rights had copied the English model and prohibited a standing army in time of peace without the consent of
their state legislatures. Five states had urged such an
amendment for the federal constitution. Some had suggested
that a two-thirds or even a three-fourths vote of members of
each house be required to approve a standing army in time
of peace. Indeed, [Virginian anti-Federalist] George Mason
had attempted to add such a proviso during the [constitutional] convention when he moved to preface the clause
granting Congress authority to organize, arm, and discipline
the militia with the words "And that the liberties of the people may be better secured against the danger of standing
armies in time of peace." A strong statement of preference for
a militia must have seemed more tactful than an expression
of distrust of the army. The Second Amendment, therefore,
stated that it was the militia, not the army, that was necessary to the security of a free state. The reference to a "well
regulated" militia was meant to encourage the federal government to keep the militia in good order.

The "Safety Valve of the Constitution"

The position of this amendment, second among the ten
amendments added to the Constitution as a Bill of Rights,
underscored its importance to contemporaries. It was no less
than the safety valve of the Constitution. It afforded the
means whereby, if parchment barriers proved inadequate,
the people could protect their liberties or alter their government. It gave to the people the ultimate power of the sword.
The *Philadelphia Federal Gazette* and *Philadelphia Evening
Post* of Thursday, June 18, 1789, in an article later reprinted
in New York and Boston, explained each of the proposed
amendments to be sent to the states for ratification. The aim
of the article that became the Second Amendment was explained this way: "As civil rulers, not having their duty to
the people duly before them, may attempt to tyrannize, and
as the military forces which must be occasionally raised to
defend our country, might pervert their power to the injury
of their fellow-citizens, the people are confirmed . . . in their
right to keep and bear their private arms."

The protection it granted was a blanket one. William Rawle, George Washington's candidate for the nation's first attorney general, described the scope of the Second Amendment's guarantee. "The prohibition," he wrote, "is general." "No clause in the constitution could by any rule of construction be conceived to give congress a power to disarm the people. Such a flagitious [infamous] attempt could only be made under some general pretence by a state legislature. But if in any blind pursuit of inordinate power, either should attempt it, this amendment may be appealed to as a restraint on both."

The Second Amendment brought the American Constitution into closer conformity with its English predecessor. In both cases, the intention was to guarantee citizens the means for self-defence and to ensure that when, in the course of time, it was necessary to raise standing armies, they would never pose a danger to the liberties of the people.

The Founders Did Not Intend to Protect Individual Gun Rights

Garry Wills

A Pulitzer Prize–winning historian and political commentator, Garry Wills is an adjunct professor of American Studies at Northwestern University. He has written biographies of several presidents and studies of larger themes in American history, including *Inventing America: Jefferson's Declaration of Independence* and *Explaining America: The Federalist.* In *A Necessary Evil: A History of American Distrust of Government,* Wills attacks the arguments of antigovernment proponents, including many gun rights advocates, as unhistorical and dangerous to democracy. In an article in the *New York Review* from which the following excerpt is taken, the author takes on the so-called standard model of Second Amendment interpretation. Under this interpretation, the founders fully intended the Second Amendment to guarantee an individual's right to own guns as a traditional American right and a necessary defense against government tyranny. Wills argues that the standard model historians misunderstand or misquote the arguments of the founders and engage in deceptive scholarship to strengthen their individual rights interpretation. Instead, he believes, the founders meant to calm fears that the central government would disarm the states.

O ver the last decade [1985–1995], an industrious band of lawyers, historians, and criminologists has created a vast outpouring of articles justifying individual gun ownership on the basis of the Second Amendment: "A well-regulated militia being necessary to the security of a free State, the right of the people to keep and bear arms shall not be infringed."

This body of commentary, much of it published in refereed law journals, has changed attitudes toward the Second Amendment. The National Rifle Association's lobbyists distribute it to legislators. Journalists like Michael Kinsley and George Will disseminate this school's views. Members of it now claim, on the basis of their work's quantity and what they believe is its quality, that scholarship on this subject is now all theirs—so that even to hold an opposing view is enough to "discredit its supporters," according to the historian Joyce Lee Malcolm. . . .

Then why is there such an air of grievance, of positive victimhood, in the writings of the "Standard Model" school? They talk of the little honor they are given, of the "mendacious" attitude of the legal establishment, of a rigidity that refuses to recognize their triumph. . . . Glenn Harlan Reynolds, in the article stating the Standard Model thesis, argues that militia extremism may be fueled by the Model's opponents, who are "treating the Constitution, too, as a preserve of the elite."

Their own reciprocating nods and citations of approval are apparently not enough for these authors. Nor is popular support enough. They still talk like [comedian] Rodney Dangerfield, getting no respect. They should ask themselves more penetratingly why this should be. Perhaps it is the quality of their arguments that makes them hard to take seriously. . . .

Poor Quality of "Standard Model" Arguments

The quality of the school's arguments can be seen in the very article that proposes the "Standard Model" as the norm of scholarship in this area. Glenn Harlan Reynolds "proves" that the Second Amendment looked to private ownership of guns by quoting Patrick Henry, in these words (and these words only): "The great object is that every man be armed. . . . Everyone who is able may have a gun."

That quotation comes from the debate over adopting the Constitution. It cannot, therefore, be concerned with the Second Amendment, which was not proposed until after the Constitution was in effect. Henry is not discussing the Amendment's text, which the Standard Model says looks to other weapons than those used by the militia (citizens' armies) of the states. Henry is talking precisely about the militia clause in the Constitution, which refers *only* to military weapons ("Congress shall have the power to provide for organizing, arming, and disciplining the militia," Article I, Section 8, Clause 16). Henry argues that federal arming of militias will either supplant or duplicate the states' arming of their own forces (the arrangement under the Articles of Confederation and in colonial times). He says that, in the case of duplication,

> Our militia shall have two sets of arms, double sets of regimentals, &c.; and thus, at a very great cost, we shall be doubly armed. The great object is that every man [of the militia] be armed. But can the people afford to pay for double sets of arms, &c? Every one who is able may have a gun. But we have learned, by experience, that, necessary as it is to have arms, and though our Assembly has, by a succession of laws for many years, endeavored to have the militia completely armed, it is still far from being the case.

The debate throughout is on ways to arm the militia. The "arms" referred to are cognate with "regimentals, etc." as military equipment. The attempts to get guns in every hand are the result of state laws for equipping the militia. Henry is saying that if the states could not do this heretofore, how is the federal government to do it?

Misuse of Quotes

Time after time, in dreary expectable ways, the quotes bandied about by Standard Model scholars turn out to be truncated, removed from context, twisted, or applied to a debate different from that over the Second Amendment. Those who would argue with them soon tire of the chase from one misquotation to another, and dismiss the whole exercise—causing the angry reaction from Standard Modelers that they are not taken seriously. The problem is that taking them seriously is precisely what undermines their claims.

Yet both the general public, which has a disposition to believe that the Second Amendment protects gun ownership, and the NRA lobby are bolstered in that view by the sheer mass of the articles now being ground out and published in journals. It is difficult to sort out all the extraneous, irrelevant, and partial material daily thrown into the debate. Even to make a beginning is difficult. One must separate what the Second Amendment says from a whole list of other matters not immediately at issue. Some argue, for instance, that there is a natural right to own guns (Blackstone is often quoted here) antecedent to the right protected by the amendment, or that such a right may be protected in other places (common law, state constitutions, statute, custom, etc.). All that could be true without affecting the original scope of the Second Amendment. One could argue for instance, that owners of property have a right to charge rental on it—but that is not the point at issue in the Third Amendment (against quartering federal troops on private property).

Military Nature of the Amendment

In order to make any progress at all, we must restrict ourselves to what, precisely, is covered by the Second Amendment. That is not hard to determine, once the irrelevant debris adrift around its every term has been cleared away. Each term exists in a discernible historic context, as does the sentence structure of the amendment.

That amendment, as [James] Madison first moved it, read:

> The right of the people to keep and bear arms shall not be infringed; a well armed and well regulated militia being the best security of a free country; but no person religiously scrupulous of bearing arms shall be compelled to render military service in person.

The whole sentence looks to military matters, the second clause giving the reason for the right's existence, and the third giving an exception to that right. The connection of the parts can be made obvious by using the same structure to describe other rights. One could say, for instance: "The right of free speech shall not be infringed; an open exchange of views giving the best security to intellectual liberty; but no person shall be free to commit libel." Every part is explained in relation to every other part. The third clause makes certain what Madison means *in this place* by "bear arms." He is not saying that Quakers, who oppose war, will not be allowed to use guns for hunting or sport.

Substitutions to Madison's Amendment

Did the changes made to Madison's proposed amendment remove it from its original (solely military) context? Only two substitutions were made in the wording—"country" became "state" and "the best security of" became "necessary to." This latter change might demote the right to bear arms by comparison with other rights (perhaps, say, free speech is the very *best* security of freedom), but it does not alter the thing being discussed. Beyond that, nothing was *added* to the text, so it could not be altered by addition. Was it altered by deletion? "Well armed and" was dropped, in drafting sessions that generally compressed the language, but "well regulated" includes "well armed." Then the whole third clause was omitted—but for a reason that still dealt with the military consequences of the sentence.

Elbridge Gerry objected to the third clause on the grounds that rulers might *declare* some people "scrupulous" and then exclude them from service—as some tended to declare Quakers ineligible for office since they take no oaths; or as Catholics were once declared incapable, without scruple, of defending a Protestant government. Gerry was clearly talking of public service, not whether Quakers should go hunting or target shooting. His objection resembles the one Samuel Johnson made to limiting militia service by the imposition of a religious oath.

A Change to Emphasize Militia

One transposition was made in Madison's sentence, but it *strengthened* the military context, as even the Standard Mod-

eler, Joyce Lee Malcolm, admits. The basis for the asserted
right was put first, as is normal in legal documents. The preamble, the "whereas," the context-establishing clause—these
set the frame for what follows: "A well regulated militia being
necessary to the security of a free State, the right of the people to keep and bear arms shall not be infringed." To use
again the parallel sentence on free speech, transposition
would produce: "An open exchange of views being necessary
to the security of intellectual liberty, the right of free speech
shall not be infringed." Such preceding declaration of intent
is found, for example, in the Constitution's copyright clause
(Article 1, Section 8, Clause 8), where the simple listing of
granted powers "to coin money . . . to declare war," etc., is
varied by a prior statement of purpose: "to promote the
progress of science and useful arts by securing for limited
times to authors and inventors . . ." The prefixed words give
the reason for, and scope of, what follows.

So nothing was added or changed that affected Madison's
original subject matter. The things removed did not change
the sentence's frame of reference. The transposition fixed the
sentence even more precisely in a military context. How,
then, did the ratification alter Madison's terms? The Standard Modelers draw on an argument made by Stephen Halbrook, an argument often cited by the NRA:

> The Senate specifically rejected a proposal to add "for
> the common defense" after "to keep and bear arms,"
> thereby precluding any construction that the right was
> restricted to militia purposes and to common defense
> against foreign aggression or domestic tyranny.

His proof of deliberate preclusion is this passage in the Senate records: "It was moved, to insert the words, 'for the common defence,' but the motion was not successful." We are
not told why the motion failed. We know the Senate was
mainly compressing and combining the amendments, not
adding to the language. There are several possible reasons
for the action, all more plausible than Halbrook's sugges-
tion that "for the common defense" would have *imported* a
military sense that is lacking without it. The military sense

is the obvious sense. It does not cease to become the obvious sense if something that *might* have been added *was* not added.

Excluding the Term "Common Defense"

The obvious reason for excluding the term "common defense" is that it could make the amendment seem to support only joint action of the state militias acting in common (shared) defense under federal control. The Articles of Confederation had used "common defense" to mean just that, and the defenders of state militias would not want to restrict themselves to that alone. The likelihood that this is the proper reason is strengthened when it is considered in relation to another change the drafters made in Madison's text, from "free country" to "free state." We are not expressly given the reason for that change, either; but most people (including Standard Modeler Malcolm) agree that the reason was to emphasize the state's separate militias, not the common defense of the country. If that is the obvious reason there, it is also the obvious reason for omitting "common defense." . . .

The Amendment Does Not Authorize Insurrection

The Standard Model finds, squirreled away in the Second Amendment, not only a private right to own guns for any purpose but a public right to oppose with arms the government of the United States. It grounds this claim in the right of insurrection, which clearly does exist whenever tyranny exists. Yet the right to *overthrow* government is not given by government. It arises when government no longer has authority. One cannot say one rebels by right of that nonexistent authority. Modern militias say the government itself instructs them to overthrow government—and wacky scholars endorse this view. They think the Constitution is so deranged a document that it brands as the greatest crime a war upon itself (in Article III: "Treason against the United States shall consist only in levying war against them . . .") and then instructs its citizens to take this up (in the Second Amendment). According to this doctrine, a well-regulated group is meant to overthrow its own regulator, and a soldier swearing to obey orders is disqualified for true militia virtue.

Gun advocates claim that a militia is meant to oppose (not assist) the standing army. But even in England the militia's role was not to fight the king's army. The point of the militias was to make it unnecessary to establish a standing army. That no longer applied when the Second Amendment was adopted, since the Constitution had already provided Congress the powers to "raise and support armies" (Article I, Section 8, Clause 12), to "provide and maintain a navy" (Clause 13), and "to make rules for the government and regulation of the land and naval forces" (Clause 14). The battle against a standing army was lost when the Constitution was ratified, and nothing in the Second Amendment as it was proposed and passed altered that. Nor did it change the Constitution's provision for using militias "to suppress insurrections" (Clause 15), not to foment them.

Yet gun advocates continue to quote from the ratification debates as if those arguments applied to the interpretation of the Second Amendment. They were aimed at the military clauses in the proposed Constitution. Patrick Henry and others did not want the Constitution to pass precisely because it would set up a standing army—and it did. . . .

Second Amendment Does Not Address Private Gun Rights

As I said at the beginning, my argument does not deny any private right to own and use firearms. Perhaps that can be defended on other grounds—natural law, common law, tradition, statute. It is certainly true that most people assumed such a right in the 1780s—so naturally, in fact, that the question was not "up" and calling for specific guarantees. All I maintain is that Madison did not address that question when drafting his amendment. When he excepted those with religious scruple, he made clear that "bear arms" meant wage war—no Quaker was to be deprived of his hunting gun.

The recent effort to find a new meaning for the Second Amendment comes from the failure of appeals to other sources as a warrant for the omnipresence of guns of all types in private hands. Easy access to all these guns is hard to justify in pragmatic terms, as a matter of social policy. Mere common law or statute may yield to common sense and specific cultural needs. That is why the gun advocates appeal, above pragmatism and common sense, to a supposed sacred right enshrined in a document Americans revere. Those advocates love to quote Sanford Levinson, who compares the admitted "social costs" of adhering to gun rights with the social costs of observing the First Amendment. We have to put up with all kinds of bad talk in the name of free talk. So we must put up with our world-record rates of homicide, suicide, and accidental shootings because, whether we like it or not, the Constitution tells us to. Well, it doesn't.

The Founders Intended Most Citizens to Be Armed

Sanford Levinson

In a controversial article University of Texas law professor Sanford Levinson chastised his fellow law professors for neglecting or misinterpreting the Second Amendment. For them, according to Levinson, the amendment is "embarrassing" because it implies at least some individual right to arms. In response, many gun control advocates stress the fact that the amendment mentions a "well-regulated militia," implying that it protects states' rights rather than gun rights. In the following excerpt, Levinson insists that use of the term *people* indicates that Second Amendment rights are individual, just as this term indicates individual rights in the First, Fourth, Ninth, and Tenth Amendments. Moreover, Levinson argues that militias, as understood by the founders, included the overwhelming majority of male citizens. In that sense, the difference between an armed militia and an armed citizenry did not really exist in the founders' vision. Instead, the citizens were the militia, and their arms were a protection against both foreign dangers and oppressive government.

I begin with the appeal to text. Recall the Second Amendment: "A well regulated Militia being necessary to the security of a free State, the right of the people to keep and bear Arms shall not be infringed." No one has ever described the Constitution as a marvel of clarity, and the Second Amendment is perhaps one of the worst drafted of all its provisions.

What is special about the Amendment is the inclusion of an opening clause—a preamble, if you will—that seems to set out its purpose. No similar clause is part of any other Amendment, though that does not, of course, mean that we do not ascribe purposes to them. It would be impossible to make sense of the Constitution if we did not engage in the ascription of purpose. Indeed, the major debates about the First Amendment arise precisely when one tries to discern a purpose, given that "literalism" is a hopelessly failing approach to interpreting it. We usually do not even recognize punishment of fraud—a classic speech act—as a free speech problem because we so sensibly assume that the purpose of the First Amendment could not have been, for example, to protect the circulation of patently deceptive information to potential investors in commercial enterprises. The sharp differences that distinguish those who would limit the reach of the First Amendment to "political" speech from those who would extend it much further, encompassing non-deceptive commercial speech, are all derived from different readings of the purpose that underlies the raw text.

A standard move of those legal analysts who wish to limit the Second Amendment's force is to focus on its "preamble" as setting out a restrictive purpose. Recall [constitutional scholar] Laurence Tribe's assertion that the purpose was to allow the states to keep their militias and to protect them against the possibility that the new national government will use its power to establish a powerful standing army and eliminate the state militias. This purposive reading quickly disposes of any notion that there is an "individual" right to keep and bear arms. The right, if such it be, is only a states's right. The consequence of this reading is obvious: the national government has the power to regulate—to the point of prohibition—private ownership of guns, since that has, by stipulation, nothing to do with preserving state militias. This is, indeed, the position of the ACLU [American Civil Liberties Union], which reads the Amendment as protecting only the right of "maintaining an effective state militia. . . . The individual's right to keep and bear arms applies only to the preservation or efficiency of a well-regulated [state] militia.

Except for lawful police and military purposes, the possession of weapons by individuals is not constitutionally protected."

This is not a wholly implausible reading, but one might ask why the Framers did not simply say something like "Congress shall have no power to prohibit state-organized and directed militias." Perhaps they in fact meant to do something else. Moreover, we might ask if ordinary readers of the late 18th Century legal prose would have interpreted it as meaning something else. The text at best provides only a starting point for a conversation. In this specific instance, it does not come close to resolving the questions posed by federal regulation of arms. Even if we accept the preamble as significant, we must still try to figure out what might be suggested by guaranteeing to "the people the right to keep and bear arms"; moreover, as we shall see presently, even the preamble presents unexpected difficulties in interpretation.

Use of the Term "the People"

One might argue (and some have) that the substantive right is one pertaining to a collective body—"the people"—rather than to individuals. Professor [Lawrence] Cress, for example, argues that state constitutions regularly use the words "man" or "person" in regard to "individual rights such as freedom of conscience," whereas the use in those constitutions of the term "the people" in regard to a right to bear arms is intended to refer to the "sovereign citizenry" collectively organized. Such an argument founders, however, upon examination of the text of the federal Bill of Rights itself and the usage there of terms "the people" in the First, Fourth, Ninth, and Tenth Amendments.

Consider that the Fourth Amendment protects "[t]he right of the people to be secure in their persons," or that the First Amendment refers to the "right of the people peaceably to assemble, and to petition the Government for a redress of grievances." It is difficult to know how one might plausibly read the Fourth Amendment as other than a protection of individual rights, and it would approach the frivolous to read the assembly and petition clause as referring only to the right of state legislators to meet and pass a remonstrance directed to Congress or the President against some government act. . . .

Although the record is suitably complicated, it seems tendentious to reject out of hand the argument that the one purpose of the Amendment was to recognize an individual's right to engage in armed self-defense against criminal conduct. Historian Robert E. Shallhope supports this view, arguing in his article "The Ideological Origins of the Second Amendment" [in the *Journal of American History*] that the Amendment guarantees individuals the right "to possess arms for their own personal defense." It would be especially unsurprising if this were the case, given the fact that the development of a professional police force (even within large American cities) was still at least half a century away at the end of the colonial period. . . . But I want now to explore a second possible purpose of the Amendment, which as a sometime political theorist I find considerably more interesting.

Assume, as Professor Cress has argued, that the Second Amendment refers to a communitarian, rather than an individual right. We are still left the task of defining the relationship between the community and the state apparatus. It is this fascinating problem to which I now turn.

Defining Militia

Consider once more the preamble and its reference to the importance of a well-regulated militia. Is the meaning of the term obvious? Perhaps we should make some effort to find out what the term "militia" meant to 18th century readers and writers. . . .

I, for one, have been persuaded that the term "militia" did not have the limited reference that Professor Cress and many modern legal analysts assign to it. There is strong evidence that "militia" refers to all of the people, or at least all of those treated as full citizens of the community. Consider, for example, the question asked by George Mason, one of the Virginians who refused to sign the Constitution because of its lack of a Bill of Rights: "Who are the militia? They consist now of the whole people." Similarly, the Federal Farmer, one of the most important Anti-Federalist opponents of the Constitution, referred to a "militia, when properly formed, [as] in fact the people themselves." We have, of course, moved now from text to history. And this history is most interesting, especially when we look at the development of notions of popular sovereignty. It has become almost a cliche of contemporary American historiography to link the development of American political thought, including its constitutional aspects, to republican thought in England, the "country" critique of the powerful "court" centered in London.

View of James Harrington

One of the school's most important writers, of course, was James Harrington, who not only was influential at the time but also has recently been given a certain pride of place by one of the most prominent of contemporary "neo-republicans,"[1] Professor Frank Michelman. One historian [Robert Shallhope] describes Harrington as having made "the most significant contribution to English libertarian attitudes toward arms, the individual, and society." He was a central figure in the development of the ideas of popular sovereignty and republicanism. For Harrington, preservation of republican liberty requires independence, which rests primarily on possession of adequate property to make men free from coercion by employers or landlords. But widespread ownership of land is not sufficient. These independent yeomen would also bear arms. As Professor [Edmund] Morgan puts it, "These independent yeomen, armed and embodied in a militia, are also a popular government's best protection against its enemies, whether they be aggressive foreign monarchs or scheming demagogues within the nation itself."

A central fear of Harrington and of all future republicans was a standing army, composed of professional soldiers. Harrington and his fellow republicans viewed a standing army as a threat to freedom, to be avoided at almost all costs. Thus, says Morgan, "A militia is the only safe form of military power that a popular government can employ; and because it is com-

1. a movement of historians and legal theorists promoting greater attention to community values over individual preferences

posed of the armed yeomanry, it will prevail over the mercenary professionals who man the armies of neighboring monarchs."

A Check on Tyranny

Scholars of the First Amendment have made us aware of the importance of John Trenchard and Thomas Gordon, whose Cato's Letters were central to the formation of the American notion of freedom of the press. That notion includes what Vincent Blasi would come to call the "checking value" of a free press, which stands as a sturdy exposer of governmental misdeeds. Consider the possibility, though, that the unlimited "checking value" in a republican polity is the ability of an armed populace, presumptively motivated by a shared commitment to the common good, to resist governmental tyranny. Indeed, one of Cato's letters refers to "the Exercise of despotick Power [as] the unrelenting War of an armed Tyrant upon his unarmed subjects . . ."

Cress persuasively shows that no one defended universal possession of arms. New Hampshire had no objection to disarming those who "are or have been in actual rebellion," just as Samuel Adams stressed that only "peaceable citizens" should be protected in their right of "keeping their own arms." All these points can be conceded, however, without conceding as well that Congress—or, for that matter, the States—had the power to disarm these "peaceable citizens."

Surely one of the foundations of American political thought of the period was the well-justified concern about political corruption and consequent governmental tyranny. Even the Federalists, fending off their opponents who accused them of foisting an oppressive new scheme upon the American people, were careful to acknowledge the risk of tyranny. James Madison, for example, speaks in Federalist Number Forty-Six of "the advantage of being armed, which the Americans possess over the people of almost every other nation." The advantage in question was not merely the defense of American borders; a standing army might well accomplish that. Rather, an armed public was advantageous in protecting political liberty. It is therefore no surprise that the

Federal Farmer, the nom de plume of an anti-federalist critic of the new Constitution and its absence of a Bill of Rights, could write that "to preserve liberty, it is essential that the whole body of the people always possess arms, and be taught alike, especially when young, how to use them . . ." On this matter, at least, there was no cleavage between the pro-ratification Madison and his opponent.

The Founders Intended to Preserve State Militias

Paul Finkelman

Many argue that the Second Amendment preserves the individual right to bear arms, both as a traditional right of the American colonists and as a defense against tyranny. University of Tulsa law professor Paul Finkelman disagrees. Instead, he believes the authors of the amendment simply meant to reassure opponents of the Constitution who worried that Congress might use a national army to overpower state governments or even create a military dictatorship. Although they denied any such intention, the framers recognized these fears and passed an amendment guaranteeing states their right to form and maintain militias, according to Finkelman. For him, the emphasis should be on the "well-regulated militia" clause of the Second Amendment. He denies that the founders meant to guarantee unlimited gun rights. Indeed, he finds this reading absurd, as it would prevent government from disarming criminals, pirates, the mentally ill, and other groups that everyone would agree should not have guns. Instead, the "right to bear arms" refers to properly organized militias under state, and ultimately under national, control.

The same men who wrote the Constitution, creating a strong central government, also wrote the bill of rights that amended the Constitution. Contrary to popular myth, the amendments were not a radical revolutionary response to the conservative constitution. The Congress of 1789, which wrote the Bill of Rights, was totally and completely

Paul Finkelman, "A Well-Regulated Militia: The Second Amendment in Historical Perspective," *The Second Amendment in Law and History,* edited by Carl T. Bogus. New York: The New Press, 2000. Copyright © 2000 by The New Press, www.thenewpress.com. Reproduced by permission.

dominated by Federalists, supporters of the Constitution, who had no desire to undermine the stability of the new government or to diminish its power. Thus, when they added amendments to the Constitution, they did so carefully, for the most part avoiding any amendments that might have subverted the powers of the new government. James Madison proudly noted that "the structure & stamina of the Govt are as little touched as possible" by the amendments he proposed. It is in this context that the Second Amendment was written, and it is in this context that it must be understood.

As Madison and the Federalists who controlled the First Congress well understood, the Second Amendment was designed to preserve the power of the national government in maintaining order, while at the same time reaffirming that the states would always have the power to organize, train, and if necessary arm their militias, so long as they were "well regulated." The framers of the Bill of Rights emphatically did not seek to undermine the power of the national government to govern, to maintain peace and "domestic tranquility," and, if necessary, to disarm the mob and suppress insurrections. . . .

Anti-Federalist Fears

Some anti-Federalists feared that the ability of the new government to nationalize the state militias was the first step toward a military dictatorship. As early as 1783 George Washington had argued for stronger national control over the militias. In his "Sentiments on a Peace Establishment," Washington argued for drawing from the state militias a select group of men, either as volunteers or draftees, who would serve in a national army. As many scholars have noted, and as his own letters show, Washington had little use for the militias, and would probably have happily seen them wither away while a trained professional army maintained the defense of the nation. Henry Knox, the secretary of war under the Articles of Confederation, proposed a less drastic form of nationalized training for the state militias, and their removal from the states, when necessary, for no more than a year at a time. However, such reforms went nowhere on the national level. Virginia tried to institute Washington's modest proposal that militia officers be chosen on the basis of ability, rather than social class and connections, but that reform fell flat on its face.

The Constitution offered a remedy for these proposals, by allowing for the nationalization of militia training and rules, and by allowing the federalization of the militias under the president's control when necessary "to execute the Laws of the Union, suppress Insurrections, and repel Invasions." But such powers truly frightened the anti-Federalists. . . .

New Hampshire Proposal

In order to placate the anti-Federalist minority, the Federalists in the New Hampshire convention endorsed twelve proposed amendments. Two of these amendments dealt with military issues. The Tenth provided "That no standing Army shall be Kept up in time of Peace unless with the consent of three fourths of the Members of each branch of Congress; nor shall Soldiers in Time of Peace be Quartered upon private Houses without the consent of the Owners." The Congress ignored the first clause, which would have led to a significant diminution of national power. On the other hand, they endorsed the second clause, and incorporated it into what became the Third Amendment.

The other military amendment proposed by New Hampshire is more interesting. The Twelfth, and last, on the New Hampshire list declared: "Congress shall never disarm any Citizen unless such as are or have been in Actual Rebellion." There are two ways we might interpret "disarm," which of course is the opposite of "keep and bear arms." If we took this to be an individual right, it would mean that Congress would have been unable to pass a federal law to disarm convicted felons, or indeed people in the process of committing a crime. . . . But if we see the language of "disarm any Citizen" as part of the notion of "bearing arms" for the militia, then the clause is suddenly reasonable and sensible. The New Hampshire Federalists are saying, in effect, that Congress cannot disarm the militias—the civilian-based armies of the states—unless they "are or have been in Actual Rebellion." On another linguistic level this is the only interpretation that makes any sense. Surely New Hampshire could not imagine a single citizen, or even a handful of malcontents, being "in Actual Rebellion." But the citizens in the militia could be. . . .

Thus the people in New Hampshire understood, from their own recent history, that the militia could turn on the government and might have to be disarmed. Yet surely they did not fear any government that could take weapons out of the hands of criminals, pirates, and the like. Thus, the only plausible understanding of New Hampshire's use of the term "disarm" is in the context of the militia.

In this context, to "keep and bear arms" is a right that is intrinsically collective: it is the right of the community to "keep and bear arms" for the purposes of maintaining a "well regulated" militia. . . .

A Collective or Individual Right?

Sanford Levinson, in a provocative article, dismisses the collective rights interpretation of the language in the Second Amendment with the clever argument that the term "people" must refer to individuals because that is how the term is used in the Fourth Amendment. This analysis, in the end, may not be terribly persuasive. He notes that the Fourth Amendment uses the term "people" but that "[i]t is difficult to know how one might plausibly read the Fourth Amendment as other than a protection of individual rights." This surely makes sense. But does it prove that the term "people" in the Second Amendment must also refer to individual rights? We certainly understand that words in the Constitution can have multiple meanings. . . .

Linguistically, then, the term "people" in the Second Amendment might be understood either way. Standing alone, the phrase "the right of the people to keep and bear arms" could apply to individuals or, collectively, to "the people." But unlike the use of the word in the Fourth Amendment, the Second Amendment ties the term "people" to a collective entity, the "well regulated Militia," which is "necessary to the security of a free State." This understanding is also supported by the original wording of the amendment, which referred to the "body" of the people. Linguistically the amendment can easily be read to be about the "body" of the people. The amendment does not say, "individually armed citizens, being necessary to the security of a free state." The Amendment explicitly refers to the "militia"—a collective organization—and a specific kind of militia at that, one that is "well regulated." It is hard to imagine individuals being "well regulated" by the government. They are only "regulated" as a group.

Levinson also poses the clever query: "One might ask why the Framers did not simply say something like 'Congress shall have no power to prohibit state-organized and directed militias.'" We might just as cleverly turn Levinson's question around. One might ask, if they had intended to protect the individual right to own weapons, why didn't the framers simply say something like, "Congress shall have no power to prohibit the private ownership of guns." Indeed, that was what the anti-Federalists in much of the country had asked for in their proposed amendments and truly *wanted* Congress to say. The fact that Madison refused to adopt such language—and that Congress did not amend the proposal to add such language—suggests that the Federalists who were in control of the Congress in 1789 did not intend to create an individual right. Indeed, they added the explanatory clause at the beginning of the amendment—"A well regulated Militia being necessary to the security of a free State"—to make certain that no one would misunderstand their intent.

The internal language of the clause also makes Levinson's reading, and that of other individual rights proponents, seem absurd. If the right to keep and bear arms "shall not be infringed," then the national government presumably has no power, in any of its many jurisdictions, to disarm anyone. A comparison with the Pennsylvania state constitution of 1776 illustrates this. That constitution says "That the people have a right to bear arms for the defense of themselves and the state; and as standing armies in the time of peace are dangerous to liberty, they should not be kept up. And that the military should be kept under strict subordination to, and governed by, the civil power."

Under the Pennsylvania state constitution, the right to bear arms "for defense of themselves" can be seen as an individual right, but it is strictly limited to self-defense. It does not give one the right to use arms to commit crimes, to intimidate others, to hunt, or even for recreational target practice. Presumably, as with most other "rights," the legislature could impose reasonable limitations on what constitutes a weapon of "defense."

Second Amendment Language Is Absolutist

Unlike the Pennsylvania constitution, the language of the Second Amendment is absolute: "shall not be infringed." If read as an individual right, criminals, convicted felons, pirates, or revolutionaries could all stand armed in the District of Columbia or in the federal territories. Pirates could load up their ships on the Potomac River and sail out to sea. Hunters could trample through Yellowstone or any other national park, guns in hand. Anyone might board a plane, gun in hand, or carry a weapon into Congress, the White House, or any other federal building. After all, what better place to exercise your Second Amendment rights than in front of your representatives or even in the courts of justice. Absurd as this would be, such people could not be "disarmed," at least until they began to commit a crime, if the Second Amendment creates an individual right to bear arms. Taken to its logical extreme, we might argue that, just as a federal felon, serving time, has some First Amendment rights to press, petition, and religion, or Eighth Amendment rights not to be subjected to cruel punishment, so too, a prisoner might claim some Second Amendment right. The Fifth Amendment allows the taking of liberty under some circumstances, while the Second, if read as an individual right, does not.

Federalist Majority Preserves National Powers

As we have seen, however, Madison and the great Federalist majority in the First Congress rejected any amendments that undermined the power of the national government. Is it conceivable that they failed to follow this philosophy with the Second Amendment? That they meant to implement the demands of the Pennsylvania anti-Federalists and, in effect, eviscerate the power of the national government? Such an argument goes against the entire history of the period.

Hence, the Second Amendment prevents Congress from abolishing the organized or "well regulated" state militias. Today such an argument may seem almost silly. Why, modern Americans might ask, would Madison bother to promise not to abolish the state militias, and why would the anti-Federalists think this was some sort of victory, or even a "tub"[1] thrown at them?

Madison and his colleagues provided for an amendment dealing with the militia because most of the states that proposed amendments wanted some guarantee that Congress would not destroy their militias. The states understood that the power to regulate might imply the power to destroy. John DeWitt, Luther Martin, and other anti-Federalists certainly feared that the national government would indeed abolish the state militias. Washington's 1783 "Sentiments on a Peace Establishment" did not call for the outright abolition of the militias, but it did call for them to take a clearly secondary role in the defense of the nation. Moreover, Washington proposed skimming the best militiamen for national service and leaving to the state militias only those "who from domestic Circumstances, bodily defects, natural awkwardness or disinclinations can never acquire the habits of Soldiers."

None of the Federalist framers saw it that way; they had no desire to destroy the state militias, just as they had no desire to impose a national church on the people, institute cruel and unusual punishments, or deny people the right against self-incrimination. A militia-protecting amendment was completely within the scope of Madison's desire to add amendments that would not affect "the structure & stamina of the Govt." He "limited" his proposed amendments "to points which are important in the eyes of many and can be objectionable in those of none." A guarantee that the states could maintain well-regulated mili-

---

1. Some anti-Federalists considered the Bill of Rights to be similar to a tub that sailors would throw out to distract a whale from attacking their ship. For them, the Constitution itself was the true danger, and the amendments were appealing distractions designed to prevent them from substantially restricting constitutional powers or even calling for a second constitutional convention.

tias—militias that remained subject to congressional control and federal deployment—did not conflict with this goal.

Significantly, Madison also limited his "tub" to the anti-Federalists by having the national government promise not to dismantle the organized, "well regulated" state militias. This phrase, "well regulated" further shows that the amendment does not apply to just anyone. It does not apply to the "unorganized" militia, because that militia is certainly not "well regulated." Nor can it apply to individual citizens who might choose to keep and bear arms "for the defense of themselves." The Pennsylvania dissenters had wanted this, but they did not get it. A new mob, led by another Daniel Shays,[2] could be disarmed by the national government. Nor does it apply to the hunter and sportsman. The majority in the First Congress intended to reassure the anti-Federalists that the national government would not disarm those who are trained by the state militia and in that body—the "well regulated militia."

Interpreting "Keep and Bear Arms"

Supporters of an individual rights interpretation of the amendment place great emphasis on the term "keep and bear arms." However, this is clearly a term of art, applied to militias in England and America, just as criminal cases at the time used the term of art "with force and arms." Beyond that, Madison wanted to reassure the states that their militias would be armed at all times. Without such a clause, Congress might allow the militias to continue, but nevertheless disarm them, thus making them impotent. This is what Great Britain had sought in 1775. The British government did not ban the colonial militias—after all, they were necessary in case of an invasion, Indian war, or rebellion. But if the militias were disarmed, as the lobster backs tried to do at Concord, they would be unable to resist British policy but could, nevertheless, be called out, and armed, to protect the empire. The battle on Lexington Green was fought to prevent the *disarming* of the local militias, not over their elimination. . . .

During the ratification debates, the proponents of the Constitution reiterated the point that Congress would be-

2. Shays was the leader of an insurrection protesting excessive taxation in 1786–1787.

come the supplier of weapons for the states. Noah Webster, for example, pointed out that Congress had the "power to provide for the organizing, arming, and disciplining the militia," although he also noted that Congress could call out the militia only under certain well-defined circumstances. Presumably, the power to "arm" the militia may also have included the power *not* to "arm" the militia. Thus, the Second Amendment guaranteed that the militias would be armed to head off the exaggerated fears of some anti-Federalists, who believed the Constitution was the prelude to a military takeover by a standing army led by the Senate and the president. Not only did the Congress lack the power to disarm the "well regulated" state militias, but if Congress failed to provide arms for them, presumably the states could appropriate money for their own arms or even order militia members to provide their own weapons.

Neither in 1787 nor in 1789 did Madison and the Federalists have any interest in disarming the state militias, just as they had no interest in imposing a national religion on the American people or in denying accused criminals the right to a jury trial. Thus, when the anti-Federalists demanded explicit protections on these and other points, Madison was willing to comply. He was not interested, however, in changing the power relations created at the Philadelphia Convention, or in undermining the nation's ability to defend itself from enemies and criminals, foreign or domestic.

The Second Amendment protected the right of the states to maintain and arm their own militias, as long as they were "well regulated" and ultimately under federal control. The Amendment was not a suicide clause allowing revolutionaries to create private militias with which to overthrow the national government or even to impede the faithful execution of the law; it prevented Congress from abolishing the organized, well-regulated militias of the states.

CHAPTER TWO

The Supreme Court Interprets the Second Amendment

The Bill of Rights

The Court Rules That the Second Amendment Applies Only to Congress

Morrison Remick Waite

In 1872 Louisiana split over a sharply contested guberna-
torial election in which two candidates claimed victory. One
candidate favored segregation of blacks; the other candidate opposed segregation. When a group of African Americans, some armed, assembled in a courthouse in support of
the anti-segregationist, a white mob, led by William Cruikshank, burned the courthouse down, shooting anyone who
tried to flee and killing one hundred black men in the
process. The mob's three ringleaders were convicted under
a federal law against interfering with a citizen's constitutional rights, including the right to assemble and the right
to bear arms. They appealed the case to the Supreme
Court. In its ruling, which freed the defendants, the Court
found that the restrictions in the Bill of Rights, including
the Second Amendment, are enforceable against Congress
but not against state governments. Much of the Court's rea-
soning has subsequently been overturned by the Court. For
example, the Court has found that many rights contained
in the Bill of Rights—including the right to freedom of
speech and freedom of religion—apply to state and local
governments as well as the federal government. However,
its decision here that the Second Amendment "has no other
purpose than to restrict the powers of the national government" has not been specifically overruled and continues to
stand as a precedent. The opinion was written by Morrison
Remick Waite, appointed chief justice by President Ulysses
S. Grant in 1874. Although he was a surprise choice after
four others turned Grant down, Waite proved an influen-

Morrison Remick Waite, majority opinion, *U.S. v. Cruikshank*, 1875.

tial justice. His opinions tended to restrict federal powers and the scope of the new Thirteenth, Fourteenth, and Fifteenth Amendments.

———————

This case comes here with a certificate by the judges of the Circuit Court for the District of Louisiana that they were divided in opinion upon a question which occurred at the hearing. It presents for our consideration an indictment containing sixteen counts, divided into two series of eight counts each, based upon sect. 6 of the Enforcement Act of May 31, 1870. That section is as follows:—

> 'That if two or more persons shall band or conspire together, or go in disguise upon the public highway, or upon the premises of another, with intent to violate any provision of this act, or to injure, oppress, threaten, or intimidate any citizen, with intent to prevent or hinder his free exercise and enjoyment of any right or privilege granted or secured to him by the constitution or laws of the United States, or because of his having exercised the same, such persons shall be held guilty of felony, and, on conviction thereof, shall be fined or imprisoned, or both, at the discretion of the court,—the fine not to exceed $5,000, and the imprisonment not to exceed ten years; and shall, moreover, be thereafter ineligible to, and disabled from holding, any office or place of honor, profit, or trust created by the constitution or laws of the United States.'

The question certified arose upon a motion in arrest of judgment after a verdict of guilty generally upon the whole sixteen counts, and is stated to be, whether 'the said sixteen counts of said indictment are severally good and sufficient in law, and contain charges of criminal matter indictable under the laws of the United States.'

The general charge in the first eight counts is that of 'banding,' and in the second eight, that of 'conspiring' together to injure, oppress, threaten, and intimidate Levi Nelson and Alexander Tillman, citizens of the United States, of

African descent and persons of color, with the intent thereby to hinder and prevent them in their free exercise and enjoyment of rights and privileges 'granted and secured' to them 'in common with all other good citizens of the United States by the constitution and laws of the United States.'

The offences provided for by the statute in question do not consist in the mere 'banding' or 'conspiring' of two or more persons together, but in their banding or conspiring with the intent, or for any of the purposes, specified. To bring this case under the operation of the statute, therefore, it must appear that the right, the enjoyment of which the conspirators intended to hinder or prevent, was one granted or secured by the constitution or laws of the United States. If it does not so appear, the criminal matter charged has not been made indictable by any act of Congress.

Federal System

We have in our political system a government of the United States and a government of each of the several States. Each one of these governments is distinct from the others, and each has citizens of its own who owe it allegiance, and whose rights, within its jurisdiction, it must protect. The same person may be at the same time a citizen of the United States and a citizen of a State, but his rights of citizenship under one of these governments will be different from those he has under the other.

Citizens are the members of the political community to which they belong. They are the people who compose the community, and who, in their associated capacity, have established or submitted themselves to the dominion of a government for the promotion of their general welfare and the protection of their individual as well as their collective rights. In the formation of a government, the people may confer upon it such powers as they choose. The government, when so formed, may, and when called upon should, exercise all the powers it has for the protection of the rights of its citizens and the people within its jurisdiction; but it can exercise no other. The duty of a government to afford protection is limited always by the power it possesses for that purpose.

Purpose of National Government

Experience made the fact known to the people of the United States that they required a national government for national purposes. The separate governments of the separate States, bound together by the articles of confederation alone, were not sufficient for the promotion of the general welfare of the people in respect to foreign nations, or for their complete protection as citizens of the confederated States. For this reason, the people of the United States, 'in order to form a more perfect union, establish justice, insure domestic tranquillity, provide for the common defence, promote the general welfare, and secure the blessings of liberty' to themselves and their posterity (Const. Preamble), ordained and established the government of the United States, and defined its powers by a constitution, which they adopted as its fundamental law, and made its rule of action.

The government thus established and defined is to some extent a government of the States in their political capacity. It is also, for certain purposes, a government of the people. Its powers are limited in number, but not in degree. Within the scope of its powers, as enumerated and defined, it is supreme and above the States; but beyond, it has no existence. It was erected for special purposes, and endowed with all the powers necessary for its own preservation and the accomplishment of the ends its people had in view. It can neither grant nor secure to its citizens any right or privilege not expressly or by implication placed under its jurisdiction.

The people of the United States resident within any State are subject to two governments: one State, and the other National; but there need be no conflict between the two. The powers which one possesses, the other does not. They are established for different purposes, and have separate jurisdictions. Together they make one whole, and furnish the people of the United States with a complete government, ample for the protection of all their rights at home and abroad. True, it may sometimes happen that a person is amenable to both jurisdictions for one and the same act. Thus, if a marshal of the United States is unlawfully resisted while executing the process of the courts within a State, and the resistance is accompanied by an assault on the officer, the sovereignty of the United States is violated by the resistance, and that of the State by the breach of peace, in the assault. So, too, if one passes counterfeited coin of the United States within a State, it may be an offence against the United States and the State: the United States, because it discredits the coin; and the State, because of the fraud upon him to whom it is passed. This does not, however, necessarily imply that the two governments possess powers in common, or bring them into conflict with each other. It is the natural consequence of a citizenship which owes allegiance to two sovereignties, and claims protection from both. The citizen cannot complain, because he has voluntarily submitted himself to such a form of government. He owes allegiance to the two departments, so to speak, and within their respective spheres must pay the penalties which each exacts for disobedience to its laws. In return, he can demand protection from each within its own jurisdiction.

Limited Powers

The government of the United States is one of delegated powers alone. Its authority is defined and limited by the Constitution. All powers not granted to it by that instrument are reserved to the States or the people. No rights can be acquired under the constitution or laws of the United States, except such as the government of the United States has the authority to grant or secure. All that cannot be so granted or secured are left under the protection of the States.

We now proceed to an examination of the indictment, to ascertain whether the several rights, which it is alleged the defendants intended to interfere with, are such as had been in law and in fact granted or secured by the constitution or laws of the United States. . . .

Second Amendment Restricts Congress

The second and tenth counts are . . . defective. The right there specified is that of 'bearing arms for a lawful purpose.' This is not a right granted by the Constitution. Neither is it in any manner dependent upon that instrument for its existence.

The second amendment declares that it shall not be infringed; but this . . . means no more than that it shall not be infringed by Congress. This is one of the amendments that has no other effect than to restrict the powers of the national government, leaving the people to look for their protection against any violation by their fellow-citizens of the rights it recognizes, to what is called, in *The City of New York v. Miln,* the 'powers which relate to merely municipal legislation, or what was, perhaps, more properly called internal police,' 'not surrendered or restrained' by the Constitution of the United States.

The third and eleventh counts are even more objectionable. They charge the intent to have been to deprive the citizens named, they being in Louisiana, 'of their respective several lives and liberty of person without due process of law.' This is nothing else than alleging a conspiracy to falsely imprison or murder citizens of the United States, being within the territorial jurisdiction of the State of Louisiana. The rights of life and personal liberty are natural rights of man. 'To secure these rights,' says the Declaration of Independence, 'governments are instituted among men, deriving their just powers from the consent of the governed.' The very highest duty of the States, when they entered into the Union under the Constitution, was to protect all persons within their boundaries in the enjoyment of these 'unalienable rights with which they were endowed by their Creator.' Sovereignty, for this purpose, rests alone with the States. It is no more the duty or within the power of the United States to punish for a conspiracy to falsely imprison or murder within a State, than it would be to punish for false imprisonment or murder itself.

The Fourteenth Amendment

The fourteenth amendment prohibits a State from depriving any person of life, liberty, or property, without due process of law; but this adds nothing to the rights of one citizen as against another. It simply furnishes an additional guaranty against any encroachment by the States upon the fundamental rights which belong to every citizen as a member of society. As was said by Mr. Justice Johnson, in *Bank of Columbia v. Okely,* it secures 'the individual from the arbitrary exercise of the powers of government, unrestrained by the established principles of private rights and distributive justice.' These counts in the indictment do not call for the exercise of any of the powers conferred by this provision in the amendment.

The fourth and twelfth counts charge the intent to have been to prevent and hinder the citizens named, who were of African descent and persons of color, in 'the free exercise and enjoyment of their several right and privilege to the full and equal benefit of all laws and proceedings, then and there, before that time, enacted or ordained by the said State of Louisiana and by the United States; and then and there, at that time, being in force in the said State and District of Louisiana aforesaid, for the security of their respective persons and property, then and there, at that time enjoyed at and within said State and District of Louisiana by white persons, being citizens of said State of Louisiana and the United States, for the protection of the persons and property of said white citizens.' There is no allegation that this was done because of the race or color of the persons conspired against. When stripped of its verbiage, the case as presented amounts to nothing more than that the defendants conspired to prevent certain citizens of the United States, being within the State of Louisiana, from enjoying the equal protection of the laws of the State and of the United States.

The fourteenth amendment prohibits a State from denying to any person within its jurisdiction the equal protection of the laws; but this provision does not, any more than the one which precedes it, and which we have just considered, add any thing to the rights which one citizen has under the Constitution against another. The equality of the rights of citizens is a principle of republicanism. Every republican government is in duty bound to protect all its citizens in the enjoyment of this principle, if within its power. That duty was originally assumed by the States; and it still remains there. The only obligation resting upon the United States is to see that the States do not deny the right. This the amendment guarantees, but no more. The power of the national government is limited to the enforcement of this guaranty. . . .

National Government Does Not Do Policing

The seventh and fifteenth counts are no better than the sixth and fourteenth. The intent here charged is to put the parties named in great fear of bodily harm, and to injure and oppress them, because, being and having been in all things qualified, they had voted 'at an election before that time had and held according to law by the people of the said State of Louisiana, in said State, to wit, on the fourth day of November, A.D. 1872, and at divers other elections by the people of the State, also before that time had and held according to law.' There is nothing to show that the elections voted at were any other than State elections, or that the conspiracy was formed on account of the race of the parties against whom the conspirators were to act. The charge as made is really of nothing more than a conspiracy to commit a breach of the peace within a State. Certainly it will not be claimed that the United States have the power or are required to do mere police duty in the States. If a State cannot protect itself against domestic violence, the United States may, upon the call of the executive, when the legislature cannot be convened, lend their assistance for that purpose. This is a guaranty of the Constitution (art. 4, sect. 4); but it applies to no case like this.

We are, therefore, of the opinion that the first, second, third, fourth, sixth, seventh, ninth, tenth, eleventh, twelfth, fourteenth, and fifteenth counts do not contain charges of a criminal nature made indictable under the laws of the United States, and that consequently they are not good and sufficient in law. They do not show that it was the intent of the defendants, by their conspiracy, to hinder or prevent the enjoyment of any right granted or secured by the Constitution.

The Second Amendment Does Not Forbid States from Regulating Arms

William Woods

In the late 1880s there was a great deal of uneasiness about immigrants and labor unrest. When Herman Presser formed a drill company for the protection of German immigrant workers, the state of Illinois charged him under an 1870 law designed to control paramilitary groups. Presser was fined ten dollars for unlicensed drilling while armed (actually, he carried a sword), and he fought this punishment all the way to the Supreme Court. Unlike *Cruikshank,* here the issue was specifically whether state governments had the power to regulate arms. The Court held that the Second Amendment did not prevent states from regulating private paramilitary organizations. At the same time, it affirmed that "all citizens capable of bearing arms constitute the reserved military force or reserve militia," indicating that states could not actually disarm their citizens. The opinion was written by Associate Justice William Woods, who served from 1881 until his death in 1887. Woods had served in the Union Army, but after the Civil War he settled in the South. He was appointed by President Rutherford B. Hayes with the support of both northern and southern senators. Generally voting with the majority, Woods wrote numerous opinions, but only two are seen as having lasting significance: *United States v. Harris* (1883), which overturned a number of federal civil rights laws, and *Presser v. State of Illinois.*

William Woods, majority opinion, *Presser v. State of Illinois,* 1886.

The position of the plaintiff in error in this court was that the entire statute under which he was convicted was invalid and void because its enactment was the exercise of a power by the legislature of Illinois forbidden to the states by the constitution of the United States. The clauses of the constitution of the United States referred to in the assignments of error were as follows:

> 'Article 1, 8. The congress shall have power . . . to raise and support armies; . . . to provide for calling forth the militia to execute the laws of the Union, suppress insurrections, and repel invasions; to provide for organizing, arming, and disciplining the militia, and for governing such part of them as may be employed in the service of the United States, reserving to the states, respectively, the appointment of the officers, and the authority of training the militia, according to the discipline prescribed by congress; . . . to make all laws which shall be necessary and proper, for carrying into execution the foregoing powers,' etc.

> 'Article 1, 10. No state shall, without the consent of congress, keep troops . . . in time of peace.'

> 'Art. 2 of Amendments. A well regulated militia being necessary to the security of a free state, the right of the people to keep and bear arms shall not be infringed.'

The plaintiff in error also contended that the enactment of the fifth and sixth sections of article 11 of the Military Code was forbidden by subdivision 3 of section 9 of article 1, which declares 'no bill of attainder or ex post facto law shall be passed,' and by article 14 of Amendments, which provides that 'no state shall make or enforce any law which shall abridge the privileges or immunities of citizens of the United States, nor shall any state deprive any person of life, liberty, or property without due process of law.'

Illinois's Military Code

The first contention of counsel for plaintiff in error is that the congress of the United States having, by virtue of the provisions of article 1 of section 8, above quoted, passed the act of May 8, 1792, entitled 'An act more effectually to provide for the national defense by establishing an uniform militia throughout the United States,' the act of February 28, 1795, 'to provide for calling forth the militia to execute the laws of the Union, suppress insurrections, and repel invasions,' and the act of July 22, 1861, 'to authorize the employment of volunteers to aid in enforcing the laws and protecting public property,' and other subsequent acts, now forming 'Title 16, The Militia,' of the Revised Statutes of the United States, the legislature of Illinois had no power to pass the act approved May 28, 1879, 'to provide for the organization of the state militia, entitled the 'Military Code of Illinois," under the provisions of which (sections 5 and 6 of article 11) the plaintiff in error was indicted.

The argument in support of this contention is, that the power of organizing, arming, and disciplining the militia being confided by the constitution to congress, when it acts upon the subject, and passes a law to carry into effect the constitutional provision, such action excludes the power of legislation by the state on the same subject.

It is further argued that the whole scope and object of the Military Code of Illinois is in conflict with that of the law of congress. It is said that the object of the act of congress is to provide for organizing, arming, and disciplining all the able-bodied male citizens of the states, respectively, between certain ages, that they may be ready at all times to respond to the call of the nation to enforce its laws, suppress insurrection, and repel invasion, and thereby avoid the necessity for maintaining a large standing army, with which liberty can never be safe, and that, on the other hand, the effect if not object of the Illinois statute is to prevent such organizing, arming, and disciplining of the militia.

Question of Universal Enrollment

The plaintiff in error insists that the act of congress requires absolutely all able-bodied citizens of the state, between certain ages, to be enrolled in the militia; that the act of Illinois makes the enrollment dependent on the necessity for the use of troops to execute the laws and suppress insurrections, and then leaves it discretionary with the governor by proclamation to require such enrollment; that the act of congress requires the entire enrolled militia of the state, with a few exemptions made by it and which may be made by state laws, to be formed into companies, battalions, regiments, brigades, and divisions; that every man shall be armed and supplied with ammunition; provides a system of discipline and field exercises for companies, regiments, etc., and subjects the entire militia of the state to the call of the president to enforce the laws, suppress insurrection, or repel invasion, and provides for the punishment of the militia officers and men who refuse obedience to his orders. On the other hand, it is said that the state law makes it unlawful for any of its able-bodied citizens, except 8,000, called the 'Illinois National Guard,' to associate themselves together as a military company, or to drill or parade with arms without the license of the governor, and declares that no military company shall leave the state with arms and equipments without his consent; that even the 8,000 men styled the 'Illinois National Guard' are not enrolled or organized as required by the act of congress, nor are they subject to the call of the president, but they constitute a military force sworn to serve in the military service of the state, to obey the orders of the governor, and not to leave the state without his consent; and that, if the state act is valid, the national act providing for organizing, arming, and disciplining the militia is of no force in the state of Illinois, for the Illinois act, so far from being in harmony with the act of congress, is an insurmountable obstacle to its execution. . . .

We are of opinion that this rule is applicable in this case. The first two sections of article 1 of the Military Code provide that all able-bodied male citizens of the state between the ages of 18 and 45 years, except those exempted, shall be subject to military duty, and be designated the 'Illinois State Militia,' and declare how they shall be enrolled and under what circumstances. The residue of the Code, except the two sections on which the indictment against the plaintiff in error is based, provides for a volunteer active militia, to consist of not more than 8,000 officers and men, declares how it shall be enlisted and brigaded, and the term of service of its officers and men; provides for brigade generals and their staffs, for the organization of the requisite battalions and companies and the election of company officers; provides for inspections, parades, and encampments, arms and armories, rifle practice, and courts-martial; provides for the pay of the officers and men, for medical service, regimental bands, books of instructions and maps; contains provisions for levying and collecting a military fund by taxation, and directs how it shall be expended; and appropriates $25,000 out of the treasury, in advance of the collection of the military fund, to be used for the purposes specified in the Military Code.

It is plain from this statement of the substance of the Military Code that the two sections upon which the indictment against the plaintiff in error is based may be separated from the residue of the Code, and stand upon their own independent provisions. These sections might have been left out of the Military Code and put in an act by themselves, and the act thus constituted and the residue of the Military Code would have been coherent and sensible acts. If it be conceded that the entire Military Code, except these sections, is unconstitutional and invalid, for the reasons stated by the plaintiff in error, these sections are separable, and, put in an act by themselves, could not be considered as forbidden by the clauses of the constitution having reference to the militia, or to the clause forbidding the states, without the consent of congress, to keep troops in time of peace. There is no such connection between the sections which prohibit any body of men, other than the organized militia of the state and the troops of the United States, from associating as a military company and drilling with arms in any city or town of the state, and the sections which provide for the enrollment and organization of the state militia, as makes it impossible to declare one, without declaring both, invalid.

This view disposes of the objection to the judgment of the supreme court of Illinois, which judgment was in effect that the legislation on which the indictment is based is not invalid by reason of the provisions of the constitution of the United States which vest congress with power to raise and support armies, and to provide for calling out, organizing, arming, and disciplining the militia, and governing such part of them as may be employed in the service of the United States, and that provision which declares that 'no state shall, without the consent of congress, . . . keep troops . . . in time of peace.'

Question of Second Amendment Violation

We are next to inquire whether the fifth and sixth sections of article 11 of the Military Code are in violation of the other provisions of the constitution of the United States relied on by the plaintiff in error. The first of these is the second amendment, which declares: 'A well regulated militia being necessary to the security of a free state, the right of the people to keep and bear arms shall not be infringed.'

We think it clear that the sections under consideration, which only forbid bodies of men to associate together as military organizations, or to drill or parade with arms in cities and towns unless authorized by law, do not infringe the right of the people to keep and bear arms. But a conclusive answer to the contention that this amendment prohibits the legislation in question lies in the fact that the amendment is a limitation only upon the power of congress and the national government, and not upon that of the state. It was so held by this court in the case of *U.S. v. Cruikshank,* in which the chief justice, in delivering the judgment of the court, said that the right of the people to keep and bear arms 'is not a right granted by the constitution.' Neither is it in any manner dependent upon that instrument for its existence. The second amendment declares that it shall not be infringed, but this, as has been seen, means no more than that it shall not be infringed by congress. This is one of the amendments that has no other effect than to restrict the powers of the national government, leaving the people to look for their protection against any violation by their fellow-citizens of the rights it recognizes to what is called in *City of New York v. Miln,* the 'powers which relate to merely municipal legislation, or what was perhaps more properly called internal police,' 'not surrendered or restrained' by the constitution of the United States.

It is undoubtedly true that all citizens capable of bearing arms constitute the reserved military force or reserve militia of the United States as well as of the states, and, in view of this prerogative of the general government, as well as of its general powers, the states cannot, even laying the constitutional provision in question out of view, prohibit the people from keeping and bearing arms, so as to deprive the United States of their rightful resource for maintaining the public security, and disable the people from performing their duty to the general government. But, as already stated, we think it clear that the sections under consideration do not have this effect.

Fourteenth Amendment

The plaintiff in error next insists that the sections of the Military Code of Illinois under which he was indicted are an invasion of that clause of the first section of the fourteenth amendment to the constitution of the United States which declares: 'No state shall make or enforce any law which shall abridge the privileges or immunities of citizens of the United States.' It is only the privileges and immunities of citizens of the United States that the clause relied on was intended to protect. A state may pass laws to regulate the privileges and immunities of its own citizens, provided that in so doing it does not abridge their privileges and immunities as citizens of the United States. The inquiry is therefore pertinent, what privilege or immunity of a citizen of the United States is abridged by sections 5 and 6 of article 11 of the Military Code of Illinois? The plaintiff in error was not a member of the organized volunteer militia of the state of Illinois, nor did he belong to the troops of the United States or to any organization under the militia law of the United States. On the contrary, the fact that he did not belong to the organized militia or the troops of the United States was an ingredient in the offense for which he was convicted and sentenced. The question is, therefore, had he a right as a citizen of the United States, in disobedience of the state law, to associate with others as a military company, and to drill and parade with arms in the towns and cities of the state? If the plaintiff in error has any such privilege, he must be able to point to the provision of the constitution or statutes of the United States by which it is conferred. . . . We have not been referred to any statute of the United States which confers upon the plaintiff in error the privilege which he asserts. The only clause in the constitution which, upon any pretense, could be said to have any relation whatever to his right to associate with others as a military company, is found in the first amendment, which declares that 'congress shall make no laws . . . abridging . . . the right of the people peaceably to assemble and to petition the government for a redress of grievances.' This is a right which it was held in *U.S. v. Cruikshank* . . . was an attribute of national citizenship, and, as such, under the protection of, and guaranteed by, the United States. But it was held in the same case that the right peaceably to assemble was not protected by the clause referred to, unless the purpose of the assembly was to petition the government for a redress of grievances. The right voluntarily to associate together as a military company or organization, or to drill or parade with arms, without, and independent of, an act of congress or law of the state authorizing the same, is not an attribute of national citizenship. Military organization and military drill and parade under arms are subjects especially under the control of the government of every country. They cannot be claimed as a right independent of law. Under our political system they are subject to the regulation and control of the state and federal governments, acting in due regard to their respective prerogatives and powers. The constitution and laws of the United States will be searched in vain for any support to the view that these rights are privileges and immunities of citizens of the United States independent of some specific legislation on the subject.

It cannot be successfully questioned that the state governments, unless restrained by their own constitutions, have the power to regulate or prohibit associations and meetings of the people, except in the case of peaceable assemblies to perform the duties or exercise the privileges of citizens of the United States, and have also the power to control and regulate the organization, drilling, and parading of military bodies and associations, except when such bodies or associations, are authorized by the militia laws of the United States. The exercise of this power by the states is necessary to the public peace, safety, and good order. . . .

The argument of the plaintiff in error that the legislation mentioned deprives him of either life, liberty, or property without due process of law, or that it is a bill of attainder or ex post facto law, is so clearly untenable as to require no discussion.

Organization of the Militia

It is next contended by the plaintiff in error that sections 5 and 6 of article 11 of the Military Code, under which he was indicted, are in conflict with the acts of congress for the organization of the militia. But this position is based on what seems to us to be an unwarranted construction of the sections referred to. It is clear that their object was to forbid voluntary military associations, unauthorized by law, from organizing or drilling and parading with arms in the cities or towns of the state, and not to interfere with the organization, arming and drilling of the militia under the authority of the acts of congress. If the object and effect of the sections were in irreconcilable conflict with the acts of congress, they would of course be invalid. But it is a rule of construction that a statute must be interpreted so as, if possible, to make it consistent with the constitution and the paramount law. If we yielded to this contention of the plaintiff in error, we should render the sections invalid by giving them a strained construction, which would make them antagonistic to the law of congress. We cannot attribute to the legislature, unless compelled to do so by its plain words, a purpose to pass an act in conflict with an act of congress on a subject over which congress is given authority by the constitution of the United States. We are, therefore, of opinion that, fairly construed, the sections of the Military Code referred to do not conflict with the laws of congress on the subject of the militia.

The plaintiff in error further insists that the organization of the Lehr und Wehr Verein [Presser's drilling company] as a corporate body, under the general corporation law of the state of Illinois, was in effect a license from the governor, within the meaning of section 5 of article 11 of the Military Code, and that such corporate body fell within the exception of the same section 'of students in educational institutions where military science is a part of the course of instruction.' In respect to these points we have to say that they present no federal question. It is not, therefore, our province to consider or decide them.

The Court Upholds a Federal Gun Control Law

James McReynolds

In the landmark 1939 case *United States v. Miller,* the Supreme Court ruled for the first time that the federal government could ban guns that are not specifically intended for militia. A convicted bank robber, Frank Miller had pleaded guilty when he was indicted for transporting a firearm in violation of the National Firearms Act of 1934, but the federal judge convinced him to withdraw his plea and ultimately ruled the act itself unconstitutional. The prosecution appealed the ruling, and the Supreme Court overruled the judge, finding that Miller's double-barreled shotgun had no obvious use in a well-regulated militia and could therefore be legally forbidden to him. In doing so, the Court came down on the side of those who say the Second Amendment guarantees states the right to maintain militias, rather than guaranteeing individuals the right to own guns. Based on numerous precedents, the Court reasoned that the primary purpose of allowing individuals to own firearms was to ensure that they could be effective militia members. In the opinion of the Court, Miller's gun did not serve this purpose. Some have argued that this ruling implies that everyone has the right to own guns that are appropriate for militia use, but that has not been the way most courts have interpreted it. The author of the opinion, Associate Justice James McReynolds, who served on the Court from 1914 to 1941, was one of the Court's most conservative members. He repeatedly voted against Franklin D. Roosevelt's New Deal programs, such as the Social Security Act. Even so, the opinion is seen as supporting the more liberal side of the gun rights debate, and it has been used by lower courts to uphold numerous gun control laws.

James McReynolds, majority opinion, *United States v. Miller,* 1939.

An indictment in the District Court Western District Arkansas, charged that Jack Miller and Frank Layton 'did unlawfully, knowingly, wilfully, and feloniously transport in interstate commerce from the town of Claremore in the State of Oklahoma to the town of Siloam Springs in the State of Arkansas a certain firearm, to-wit, a double barrel 12-gauge Stevens shotgun having a barrel less than 18 inches in length, in interstate commerce as aforesaid, not having registered said firearm as required by Section 1132d of Title 26, United States Code, 26 U.S.C.A. 1132d, and not having in their possession a stamp-affixed written order for said firearm as provided by Section 1132c, Title 26, United States Code, 26 U.S.C.A. 1132c and the regulations issued under authority of the said Act of Congress known as the 'National Firearms Act' approved June 26, 1934, contrary to the form of the statute in such case made and provided, and against the peace and dignity of the United States.' A duly interposed demurrer alleged: The National Firearms Act is not a revenue measure but an attempt to usurp police power reserved to the States, and is therefore unconstitutional. Also, it offends the inhibition of the Second Amendment to the Constitution, U.S.C.A.—'A well regulated Militia, being necessary to the security of a free State, the right of the people to keep and bear Arms, shall not be infringed.' The District Court held that section 11 of the Act violates the Second Amendment. It accordingly sustained the demurrer and quashed the indictment.

The cause is here by direct appeal.

In the absence of any evidence tending to show that possession or use of a 'shotgun having a barrel of less than eighteen inches in length' at this time has some reasonable relationship to the preservation or efficiency of a well regulated militia, we cannot say that the Second Amendment guarantees the right to keep and bear such an instrument. Certainly it is not within judicial notice that this weapon is any part of the ordinary military equipment or that its use could contribute to the common defense.

The Constitution as originally adopted granted to the Congress power—'To provide for calling forth the Militia to execute the Laws of the Union, suppress Insurrections and repel Invasions; To provide for organizing, arming, and disciplining, the Militia, and for governing such Part of them as may be employed in the Service of the United States, reserving to the States respectively, the Appointment of the Officers, and the Authority of training the Militia according to the discipline prescribed by Congress.' With obvious purpose to assure the continuation and render possible the effectiveness of such forces the declaration and guarantee of the Second Amendment were made. It must be interpreted and applied with that end in view.

Militia

The Militia which the States were expected to maintain and train is set in contrast with Troops which they were forbidden to keep without the consent of Congress. The sentiment of the time strongly disfavored standing armies; the common view was that adequate defense of country and laws could be secured through the Militia—civilians primarily, soldiers on occasion.

The signification attributed to the term Militia appears from the debates in the Convention, the history and legislation of Colonies and States, and the writings of approved commentators. These show plainly enough that the Militia comprised all males physically capable of acting in concert for the common defense. 'A body of citizens enrolled for military discipline.' And further, that ordinarily when called for service these men were expected to appear bearing arms supplied by themselves and of the kind in common use at the time.

[Legal scholar William] Blackstone's *Commentaries* points out 'that king Alfred first settled a national militia in this kingdom' and traces the subsequent development and use of such forces.

[Economist] Adam Smith's *Wealth of Nations* contains an extended account of the Militia. It is there said: 'Men of republican principles have been jealous of a standing army as dangerous to liberty.' 'In a militia, the character of the labourer, artificer, or tradesman, predominates over that of the soldier: in a standing army, that of the soldier predominates over every other character; and in this distinction seems to consist the essential difference between those two different species of military force.'

'The American Colonies In The 17th Century' [an article by Herbert L.] Osgood, Vol. 1, ch. XIII, affirms in reference to the early system of defense in New England:

> 'In all the colonies, as in England, the militia system was based on the principle of the assize of arms. This implied the general obligation of all adult male inhabitants to possess arms, and, with certain exceptions, to cooperate in the work of defence.' 'The possession of arms also implied the possession of ammunition, and the authorities paid quite as much attention to the latter as to the former.' 'A year later (1632) it was ordered that any single man who had not furnished himself with arms might be put out to service, and this became a permanent part of the legislation of the colony (Massachusetts).'

Also 'Clauses intended to insure the possession of arms and ammunition by all who were subject to military service appear in all the important enactments concerning military affairs.' Fines were the penalty for delinquency, whether of towns or individuals. According to the usage of the times, the infantry of Massachusetts consisted of pikemen and musketeers. The law, as enacted in 1649 and thereafter, provided that each of the former should be armed with a pike, corselet, head-piece, sword, and knapsack. The musketeer should carry a 'good fixed musket,' not under bastard musket bore, not less than three feet, nine inches, nor more than four feet three inches in length, a priming wire, scourer, and mould, a sword, rest, bandoleers, one pound of powder, twenty bullets, and two fathoms of match. The law also required that two-thirds of each company should be musketeers.'

Early State Ordinances

The General Court of Massachusetts, January Session 1784, provided for the organization and government of the Militia.

It directed that the Train Band should 'contain all able bodied men, from sixteen to forty years of age, and the Alarm List, all other men under sixty years of age, . . .' Also, 'That every non-commissioned officer and private soldier of the said militia not under the controul of parents, masters or guardians, and being of sufficient ability therefor in the judgment of the Selectmen of the town in which he shall dwell, shall equip himself, and be constantly provided with a good fire arm, &c.'

By an Act passed April 4, 1786, the New York Legislature directed: 'That every able-bodied Male Person, being a Citizen of this State, or of any of the United States, and residing in this State, (except such Persons as are herein after excepted) and who are of the Age of Sixteen, and under the Age of Forty-five Years, shall, by the Captain or commanding Officer of the Beat in which such Citizens shall reside, within four Months after the passing of this Act, be enrolled in the Company of such Beat. . . . That every Citizen so enrolled and notified, shall, within three Months thereafter, provide himself, at his own Expense, with a good Musket or Firelock, a sufficient Bayonet and Belt, a Pouch with a Box therein to contain not less than Twenty-four Cartridges suited to the Bore of his Musket or Firelock, each Cartridge containing a proper Quantity of Powder and Ball, two spare Flints, a Blanket and Knapsack; . . .'

The General Assembly of Virginia, October, 1785, declared: 'The defense and safety of the commonwealth depend upon having its citizens properly armed and taught the knowledge of military duty.'

It further provided for organization and control of the Militia and directed that 'All free male persons between the ages of eighteen and fifty years,' with certain exceptions, 'shall be inrolled or formed into companies.' 'There shall be a private muster of every company once in two months.'

Also that 'Every officer and soldier shall appear at his respective muster-field on the day appointed, by eleven o'clock in the forenoon, armed, equipped, and accoutred, as follows: . . . every non-commissioned officer and private with a good, clean musket carrying an ounce ball, and three feet eight

inches long in the barrel, with a good bayonet and iron ram-
rod well fitted thereto, a cartridge box properly made, to contain and secure twenty cartridges fitted to his musket, a good
knapsack and canteen, and moreover, each non-commissioned
officer and private shall have at every muster one pound of
good powder, and four pounds of lead, including twenty blind
cartridges; and each serjeant shall have a pair of moulds fit to
cast balls for their respective companies, to be purchased by
the commanding officer out of the monies arising on delinquencies. Provided, That the militia of the counties westward
of the Blue Ridge, and the counties below adjoining thereto,
shall not be obliged to be armed with muskets, but may have
good rifles with proper accoutrements, in lieu thereof. And
every of the said officers, non-commissioned officers, and pri-
vates, shall constantly keep the aforesaid arms, accoutrements, and ammunition, ready to be produced whenever
called for by his commanding officer. If any private shall make
it appear to the satisfaction of the court hereafter to be appointed for trying delinquencies under this act that he is so
poor that he cannot purchase the arms herein required, such
court shall cause them to be purchased out of the money arising from delinquents.'

State Regulations

Most if not all of the States have adopted provisions touching
the right to keep and bear arms. Differences in the language
employed in these have naturally led to somewhat variant
conclusions concerning the scope of the right guaranteed. But
none of them seem to afford any material support for the
challenged ruling of the court below.

In the margin some of the more important opinions and
comments by writers are cited. We are unable to accept the
conclusion of the court below and the challenged judgment
must be reversed. The cause will be remanded for further
proceedings.

Reversed and remanded.

Banning Convicted Felons from Owning Guns Is Constitutional

Harry Blackmun

In 1961 George Calvin Lewis pleaded guilty to breaking and entering and was imprisoned. In 1977, after serving his sentence, he was arrested for being a felon in possession of a firearm. However, his lawyer argued that his original conviction was illegal under *Gideon v. Wainwright,* the 1963 decision in which the Court held that defendants in felony cases had an absolute right to a lawyer. If the defendant wants a lawyer and cannot afford one, the government is obligated to provide one. Because Lewis had not had access to counsel in his first trial, his lawyer argued that his original conviction should be treated as unconstitutional. By that logic, Lewis could not be treated as a convicted felon, and therefore the law preventing felons from owning guns did not apply to him. In the *Lewis* decision, the Court acknowledged that the *Gideon* decision could be used to limit the scope of felony convictions in some cases. However, it did not agree that this limit applied to the possession of firearms. Focusing on the legislative history and the actual language of the statute, the Court found that Congress meant to bar any convicted felon from owning a firearm, regardless of whether that conviction was subsequently open to legal challenge or even overturned. In doing so, the Court reaffirmed Congress's right to keep arms out of the hands of criminals, noting in a footnote that "legislative restrictions on the use of firearms do not trench upon any constitutionally protected liberties."

The opinion in the 6-3 decision was written by Associate Justice Harry Blackmun. Appointed by President Richard

Harry Blackmun, majority opinion, *Lewis v. United States,* 1980.

Nixon in 1970, Blackmun was initially seen as a conservative Republican, but he was often identified with liberal positions after writing the majority opionion in *Roe v. Wade*
(1973), which found antiabortion laws unconstitutional.

This case presents the question whether a defendant's ex-
tant prior conviction, flawed because he was without
counsel, as required by *Gideon v. Wainwright,* may constitute the predicate for a subsequent conviction under 1202 (a)
(1), as amended, of Title VII of the Omnibus Crime Control
and Safe Streets Act of 1968.

In 1961, petitioner George Calvin Lewis, Jr., upon his plea
of guilty, was convicted in a Florida state court of a felony for
breaking and entering with intent to commit a misdemeanor.
He served a term of imprisonment. That conviction has never
been overturned, nor has petitioner ever received a qualifying pardon or permission from the Secretary of the Treasury
to possess a firearm.

In January 1977, Lewis, on probable cause, was arrested
in Virginia, and later was charged by indictment with having knowingly received and possessed at that time a specified firearm, in violation of 18 U.S.C. App. 1202 (a) (1). He
waived a jury and was given a bench trial. It was stipulated
that the weapon in question had been shipped in interstate
commerce. The Government introduced in evidence an exem-
plified copy of the judgment and sentence in the 1961 Florida
felony proceeding.

Objection Based on *Gideon*

Shortly before the trial, petitioner's counsel informed the
court that he had been advised that Lewis was not repre-
sented by counsel in the 1961 Florida proceeding. He claimed
that under *Gideon v. Wainwright,* a violation of 1202 (a) (1)
could not be predicated on a prior conviction obtained in violation of petitioner's Sixth and Fourteenth Amendment
rights. The court rejected that claim, ruling that the constitutionality of the outstanding Florida conviction was imma-
terial with respect to petitioner's status under 1202 (a) (1) as

a previously convicted felon at the time of his arrest. Petitioner, accordingly, offered no evidence as to whether in fact he had been convicted in 1961 without the aid of counsel. We therefore assume, for present purposes, that he was without counsel at that time.

On appeal, the United States Court of Appeals for the Fourth Circuit, by a divided vote, affirmed. It held that a defendant, purely as a defense to a prosecution under 1202 (a) (1), could not attack collaterally an outstanding prior felony conviction, and that the statutory prohibition applied irrespective of whether that prior conviction was subject to collateral attack. The Court of Appeals also rejected Lewis' constitutional argument to the effect that the use of the prior conviction as a predicate for his prosecution under 1202 (a) (1) violated his rights under the Fifth and Sixth Amendments.

Because of conflict among the Courts of Appeals, we granted certiorari.

Relevant Cases

Four cases decided by this Court provide the focus for petitioner's attack upon his conviction. The first, and pivotal one, is *Gideon v. Wainwright,* where the Court held that a state felony conviction without counsel, and without a valid waiver of counsel, was unconstitutional under the Sixth and Fourteenth Amendments. That ruling is fully retroactive.

The second case is *Burgett v. Texas* (1967). There the Court held that a conviction invalid under *Gideon* could not be used for enhancement of punishment under a State's recidivist statute. The third is *United States v. Tucker* (1972), where it was held that such a conviction could not be considered by a court in sentencing a defendant after a subsequent conviction. And the fourth is *Loper v. Beto* (1972), where the Court disallowed the use of the conviction to impeach the general credibility of the defendant. The prior conviction, the plurality opinion said, "lacked reliability."

We, of course, accept these rulings for purposes of the present case. Petitioner's position, however, is that the four cases require a reversal of his conviction under 1202 (a) (1) on both statutory and constitutional grounds.

The Language of the Statute

The Court has stated repeatedly of late that in any case concerning the interpretation of a statute the "starting point" must be the language of the statute itself. *Reiter v. Sonotone Corp.,* (1979). An examination of 1202 (a) (1) reveals that its proscription is directed unambiguously at any person who "has been convicted by a court of the United States or of a State . . . of a felony." No modifier is present, and nothing suggests any restriction on the scope of the term "convicted." "Nothing on the face of the statute suggests a congressional intent to limit its coverage to persons [whose convictions are not subject to collateral attack]." *United States v. Culbert* (1978). The statutory language is sweeping, and its plain meaning is that the fact of a felony conviction imposes a firearm disability until the conviction is vacated or the felon is relieved of his disability by some affirmative action, such as a qualifying pardon or a consent from the Secretary of the Treasury. The obvious breadth of the language may well reflect the expansive legislative approach revealed by Congress' express findings and declarations, in 18 U.S.C. App. 1201, concerning the problem of firearm abuse by felons and certain specifically described persons.

Other provisions of the statute demonstrate and reinforce its broad sweep. Section 1203 enumerates exceptions to 1202 (a) (1) (a prison inmate who by reason of his duties has expressly been entrusted with a firearm by prison authority; a person who has been pardoned and who has expressly been authorized to receive, possess, or transport a firearm). In addition, 1202 (c) (2) defines "felony" to exclude certain state crimes punishable by no more than two years' imprisonment. No exception, however, is made for a person whose outstanding felony conviction ultimately might turn out to be invalid for any reason. On its face, therefore, 1202 (a) (1) contains nothing by way of restrictive language. It thus stands in contrast with other federal statutes that explicitly permit a defendant to challenge, by way of defense, the validity or constitutionality of the predicate felony.

When we turn to the legislative history of 1202 (a) (1), we find nothing to suggest that Congress was willing to allow a defendant to question the validity of his prior conviction as a defense to a charge under 1202 (a) (1). . . .

No Basis for a Loophole

The legislative history, therefore, affords no basis for a loophole, by way of a collateral constitutional challenge, to the broad statutory scheme enacted by Congress. Section 1202 (a) was a sweeping prophylaxis, in simple terms, against misuse of firearms. There is no indication of any intent to require the Government to prove the validity of the predicate conviction.

The very structure of the Omnibus Act's Title IV, enacted simultaneously with Title VII, reinforces this conclusion. Each Title prohibits categories of presumptively dangerous persons from transporting or receiving firearms. Actually, with regard to the statutory question at issue here, we detect little significant difference between Title IV and Title VII. Each seeks to keep a firearm away from "any person . . . who has been convicted" of a felony, although the definition of "felony" differs somewhat in the respective statutes. But to limit the scope of 922 (g) (1) and (h) (1) to a validly convicted felon would be at odds with the statutory scheme as a whole. Those sections impose a disability not only on a convicted felon but also on a person under a felony indictment, even if that person subsequently is acquitted of the felony charge. Since the fact of mere indictment is a disabling circumstance, a fortiori the much more significant fact of conviction must deprive the person of a right to a firearm.

With the face of the statute and the legislative history so clear, petitioner's argument that the statute nevertheless should be construed so as to avoid a constitutional issue is inapposite. That course is appropriate only when the statute provides a fair alternative construction. This statute could not be more plain. . . .

We therefore hold that 1202 (a) (1) prohibits a felon from possessing a firearm despite the fact that the predicate felony may be subject to collateral attack on constitutional grounds.

Rational Basis

The firearm regulatory scheme at issue here is consonant with the concept of equal protection embodied in the Due Process Clause of the Fifth Amendment if there is "some 'rational basis' for the statutory distinction made . . . or . . . they 'have some relevance to the purpose for which the classification is made.'" *Marshall v. United States* (1974).

Section 1202 (a) (1) clearly meets that test. Congress, as its expressed purpose in enacting Title VII reveals, was concerned that the receipt and possession of a firearm by a felon constitutes a threat, among other things, to the continued and effective operation of the Government of the United States. The legislative history of the gun control laws discloses Congress' worry about the easy availability of firearms, especially to those persons who pose a threat to community peace. And Congress focused on the nexus between violent crime and the possession of a firearm by any person with a criminal record. Congress could rationally conclude that any felony conviction, even an allegedly invalid one, is a sufficient basis on which to prohibit the possession of a firearm. This Court has recognized repeatedly that a legislature constitutionally may prohibit a convicted felon from engaging in activities far more fundamental than the possession of a firearm. . . .

We recognize, of course, that under the Sixth Amendment an uncounseled felony conviction cannot be used for certain purposes. The Court, however, has never suggested that an uncounseled conviction is invalid for all purposes. . . .

Use of an uncounseled felony conviction as the basis for imposing a civil firearms disability, enforceable by a criminal sanction, is not inconsistent with *Burgett, Tucker,* and *Loper.* In each of those cases, this Court found that the subsequent conviction of sentence violated the Sixth Amendment because it depended upon the reliability of a past uncounseled conviction. The federal gun laws, however, focus not on reliability, but on the mere fact of conviction, or even indictment, in order to keep firearms away from potentially dangerous persons. Congress' judgment that a convicted felon, even one whose conviction was allegedly uncounseled, is among the class of persons who should be disabled from dealing in or possessing firearms because of potential dangerousness is rational. Enforcement of that essentially civil disability through a criminal sanction does not "support guilt or enhance punishment." See *Burgett,* on the basis of a conviction that is unreliable when one considers Congress' broad purpose. Moreover, unlike the situation in *Burgett,* the sanction imposed by 1202 (a) (1) attaches immediately upon the defendant's first conviction.

Again, it is important to note that a convicted felon may challenge the validity of a prior conviction or otherwise remove his disability, before obtaining a firearm. We simply hold today that the firearms prosecution does not open the predicate conviction to a new form of collateral attack. . . .

The judgment of the Court of Appeals is affirmed.

The Supreme Court's Decisions Point Away from Individual Gun Rights

Michael C. Dorf

Michael C. Dorf is a professor of law and vice dean at Columbia University's School of Law. In reviewing the Supreme Court's major Second Amendment rulings, he finds that overall the Court has interpreted the Amendment as supporting the right of states to maintain militias. In practical terms, that means that both the federal and state governments have the right to limit gun ownership by individuals. Some advocates of individual gun rights have pointed to the Court's decision in *United States v. Miller* as support for their position. This case involved a man who was convicted for possession of a sawed-off shotgun in violation of the National Firearms Act of 1934. The Court upheld the conviction on the grounds that a sawed-off shotgun was not a proper weapon in a "well-regulated militia." For some, this implies that individuals do have a right to possess weapons with proper military applications. Although Dorf agrees that the *Miller* decision might be open to this reading, he concludes that the history of gun control and the Supreme Court's decisions weigh heavily against this interpretation.

T he Supreme Court has never upheld an individual's Second Amendment objection to prosecution under a law regulating firearms. Two nineteenth-century decisions, *United States v. Cruikshank* and *Presser v. Illinois,* held that the Second Amendment does not apply to the states. Although these decisions postdated the enactment of the Fourteenth Amendment, they predated the modern cases holding that the Fourteenth Amendment incorporates most of the provisions of the Bill of Rights.[1] To the extent that *Cruikshank* and *Presser* simply rely on the old view that the Bill of Rights does not apply to the states, they might appropriately be reexamined. This does not, of course, mean that the Second Amendment necessarily applies to the states. Upon reexamination, we might conclude, for example, that the Second Amendment prohibits the federal government from asserting some measure of control over state units of the National Guard; such a limit on the federal government for the *benefit* of the states could not readily be applied *against* the states. On the other hand, if the Second Amendment protects a right of individual firearm ownership against federal interference, there would be no analytical difficulty in applying a parallel limit against the states.

What *Miller* Meant

The leading case involving the Second Amendment as a limit on federal action is *United States v. Miller.* There the Court rejected the claim that the Second Amendment protected a private right to possess a sawed-off shotgun because there was no evidence that such possession bore "some reasonable relationship to the preservation or efficiency of a well regulated militia."

Individual rights scholars correctly point out that *Miller* might plausibly be read to suggest a negative pregnant: "if the sawed-off shotgun had been a militia weapon, then," on this reading, the defendants "would have had a constitutional right to possess it." By further implication, in general, individuals would have a Second Amendment right to private possession of whatever weapons might be useful in military service. *Miller* approvingly describes state statutes in force at the time of the adoption of the federal Constitution

---

1. Originally, the Bill of Rights was interpreted to limit only the actions of the federal government. Beginning in the early twentieth century, the Supreme Court began "incorporating" many of the provisions of the Bill of Rights, which meant state laws could be ruled unconstitutional for violating these provisions. The Court has never incorporated the entire Bill of Rights, nor has it incorporated the Second Amendment.

organizing militias out of the (adult white male) citizens, who (according to the statutes) were to bring their own weapons when called to muster. When not called to muster, the argument goes, the people are entitled to, in the terms of the Second Amendment, "keep" their weapons.

Miller itself does not exclude this possibility; but neither does *Miller* compel it. Indeed, we extrapolate from the logic of *Miller* at our peril, because, under modern conditions, it would seem to grant the most constitutional protection to just those weapons that are least suitable to private possession—distinctly military "arms" such as tanks, attack helicopters, rocket launchers, or even nuclear weapons.

No Individual Rights Implication

More important, the Supreme Court has not read *Miller* to imply anything resembling an individual right to firearms possession. For example, in a 1980 case, *Lewis v. United States,* the Court upheld a federal statute prohibiting a convicted felon from possessing firearms. If the Court had been interested in safeguarding an individual right of firearms possession for law-abiding citizens, it could have relied on the fact that prohibitions on firearms possession by felons date back to colonial times. Yet the *Lewis* Court went considerably further in undermining constitutional protection for an individual right. It cited *Miller* for the proposition that the statute at issue did not "trench upon any constitutionally protected liberties."

Or consider *Adams v. Williams,* which rejected a Fourth Amendment challenge to a "stop-and-frisk" based on an informant's tip that the defendant was in illegal possession of narcotics and a handgun. Dissenting, Justice [William O.] Douglas, joined by Justice [Thurgood] Marshall, argued that the danger to the police in street encounters with suspects stemmed not from the niceties of the Fourth Amendment but from the state's failure to enact strict gun control laws. Citing *Miller,* Justice Douglas opined that "[t]here is no reason why all pistols should not be barred to everyone except the police." No member of the Court took issue with this statement.

Support for Collective Rights View

These decisions suggest that, without directly facing the question, the Supreme Court has come to understand *Miller* as standing roughly for the collective rights view of the Second Amendment. With one recent exception, the lower federal courts have also understood *Miller* this way. As a matter of doctrine, the most that can be said for reading the Second Amendment as conferring an individual right to own and carry firearms is that constitutional precedent does not pose an insuperable obstacle to that reading, although its adoption would mark a substantial change in the prevailing view, and presumably would have to satisfy the criteria ordinarily thought to justify a departure from precedent.

Answering Objections

Before moving to textual arguments, I should consider an objection to the conclusion that existing precedents stand against the individual rights view: *Miller* did not actually hold that the Second Amendment protects no individual right to firearms possession, so cases or individual opinions treating *Miller* as if it did are not entitled to the weight of precedent. This is not a trivial objection; however, and this is the point I wish to emphasize, the objection applies to much more than Second Amendment jurisprudence. For example, much of the rationale for the Supreme Court's decision in *Brown v. Board of Education* rested on an examination of the harms caused by racial segregation in *education;* yet the Court, without explanation, rapidly applied *Brown* to invalidate racial segregation in a wide variety of other contexts.

Nor has this process of precedent setting without judicial opinion been confined to the *expansion* of individual rights. As in the interpretation of the Second Amendment so, too, have First Amendment rights been *restricted* to less than they might have been by somewhat unreflective citation. For example, current First Amendment law affords less protection to labor picketing than to otherwise comparable speech outside the labor context. The difference in treatment is essentially a historical legacy: labor decisions predating modern free speech doctrine continue to be cited as good law, and, for that reason, remain good law. Furthermore, as Justice [Anthony] Kennedy has noted, even the now canonical view that content-based regulation of speech can be justified if strictly necessary to further a compelling state interest came into being by a series of sloppy citations. Yet despite his well-documented protest, Justice Kennedy convinced none of his colleagues to reexamine the test.

Power of Precedent

These examples illustrate a quite basic point that the objection under consideration ignores: the force of doctrine qua doctrine does not rest on how it came into being any more than it rests upon the soundness of the arguments that can be advanced for it. The main point of following precedent is to follow it when there is a plausible argument that it is wrong. There are, of course, occasions when constitutional precedents are abandoned because they are very clearly wrong or because they have become unworkable, and some (including me) have argued that the Supreme Court should be willing to reexamine its precedents more frequently than it does. But as a matter of precedent understood in the conventional way, the case for the individual rights view of the Second Amendment remains a very weak one. To put the matter in lawyerly terms, champions of the individual rights view of the Second Amendment must satisfy a heavy burden of persuasion. They must make an overwhelming rather than a just barely convincing case for their view.

CHAPTER THREE

Perspectives on Gun Rights and Gun Control

The Bill of Rights

Second Amendment Rights Are Essential for Liberty

Charlton Heston

Well known as the actor who played Moses in the movie *The Ten Commandments* and the title character in *Ben Hur,* Charlton Heston became the leading voice for gun rights when he joined the board of the National Rifle Association in 1997. He became the organization's president in 1998 and served in that role until 2003. In a speech to the National Press Club in 1997, he laid out his view that Second Amendment rights were fundamental in protecting liberty itself and that the amendment should be ranked first in the Bill of Rights. He also chided the press for its bias against gun rights.

Today I want to talk to you about guns: Why we have them, why the Bill of Rights guarantees that we can have them, and why my right to have a gun is more important than your right to rail against it in the press.

I believe every good journalist needs to know why the Second Amendment must be considered more essential than the First Amendment. This may be a bitter pill to swallow, but the right to keep and bear arms is not archaic. It's not an outdated, dusty idea some old dead white guys dreamed up in fear of the Redcoats. No, it is just as essential to liberty today as it was in 1776. These words may not play well at the Press Club, but it's still the gospel down at the corner bar and grill.

And your efforts to undermine the Second Amendment, to deride it and degrade it, to readily accept diluting it and eagerly promote redefining it, threaten not only the physical well-being of millions of Americans but also the core concept of individual liberty our founding fathers struggled to perfect and protect.

So now you know what doubtless does not surprise you. I believe strongly in the right of every law-abiding citizen to keep and bear arms, for what I think are good reasons.

Bill of Rights and Individual Protections

The original amendments we refer to as the Bill of Rights contain ten of what the constitutional framers termed unalienable rights. These rights are ranked in random order and are linked by their essential equality. The Bill of Rights came to us with blinders on. It doesn't recognize color, or class, or wealth. It protects not just the rights of actors, or editors, or reporters, but extends even to those we love to hate.

That's why the most heinous criminals have rights until they are convicted of a crime. The beauty of the Constitution can be found in the way it takes human nature into consideration. We are not a docile species capable of co-existing within a perfect society under everlasting benevolent rule. We are what we are. Egotistical, corruptible, vengeful, sometimes even a bit power mad. The Bill of Rights recognizes this and builds the barricades that need to be in place to protect the individual.

You, of course, remain zealous in your belief that a free nation must have a free press and free speech to battle injustice, unmask corruption and provide a voice for those in need of a fair and impartial forum.

I agree wholeheartedly . . . a free press is vital to a free society. But I wonder: How many of you will agree with me that the right to keep and bear arms is not just equally vital, but the most vital to protect all the other rights we enjoy?

Second Amendment Is Most Important

I say that the Second Amendment is, in order of importance, the first amendment. It is America's First Freedom, the one right that protects all the others. Among freedom of speech, of the press, of religion, of assembly, of redress of grievances, it is the first among equals. It alone offers the absolute capacity to live without fear. The right to keep and bear arms is the one right that allows "rights" to exist at all.

Either you believe that, or you don't, and you must decide.

Because there is no such thing as a free nation where police and military are allowed the force of arms but individual citizens are not. That's a "big brother knows best" theater of the absurd that has never boded well for the peasant class, the working class, or even for reporters.

Yes, our Constitution provides the doorway for your news and commentary to pass through free and unfettered. But that doorway to freedom is framed by the muskets that stood between a vision of liberty and absolute anarchy at a place called Concord Bridge. Our revolution began when the British sent Redcoats door to door to confiscate the people's guns. They didn't succeed: The muskets went out the back door with their owners.

[Essayist Ralph Waldo] Emerson said it best:

By the rude bridge that arched the flood,

Their flag to April's breeze unfurled,

Here once the embattled farmers stood,

And fired the shot heard round the world.

Liberty Versus Gun Control

King George called us "rabble in arms." But with God's grace, George Washington and many brave men gave us our country. Soon after, God's grace and a few great men gave us our Constitution. It's been said that the creation of the United States is the greatest political act in history. I'll sign that.

In the next two centuries, though, freedom did not flourish. The next revolution, the French, collapsed in the bloody Terror, then Napoleon's tyranny. There's been no shortage of dictators since, in many countries. Hitler, Mussolini, Stalin, Mao, Idi Amin, Castro, Pol Pot. All these monsters began by confiscating private arms, then literally soaking the earth with the blood of tens and tens of millions of their people.

Ah, the joys of gun control.

Failures of the Press

Now, I doubt any of you would prefer a rolled up newspaper as a weapon against a dictator or a criminal intruder. Yet in essence that is what you have asked our loved ones to do, through an ill-contrived and totally naive campaign against the Second Amendment.

Besides, how can we entrust to you the Second Amendment, when you are so stingy with your own First Amendment?

I say this because of the way, in recent days, you have treated your own—those journalists you consider the least among you. How quick you've been to finger the paparazzi with blame and to eye the tabloids with disdain. How eager you've been to draw a line where there is none, to demand some distinction within the First Amendment that sneers "they are not one of us." How readily you let your lesser brethren take the fall, as if their rights were not as worthy, and their purpose not as pure, and their freedom not as sacred as yours.

So now, as politicians consider new laws to shackle and gag paparazzi, who among you will speak up? Who here will stand and defend them? If you won't, I will. Because you do not define the First Amendment. It defines you. And it is bigger than you—big enough to embrace all of you, plus all those you would exclude.

That's how freedom works.

Media Is Gullible

It also demands you do your homework. Again and again I hear gun owners say, how can we believe anything the anti-gun media says when they can't even get the facts right? For too long you have swallowed manufactured statistics and fabricated technical support from anti-gun organizations that wouldn't know a semiauto from a sharp stick. And it shows. You fall for it every time.

That's why you have very little credibility among 70 million gun owners and 20 million hunters and millions of veterans who learned the hard way which end the bullet comes out. And while you attacked the amendment that defends your homes and protects your spouses and children, you have denied those of us who defend all the Bill of Rights a fair hearing or the courtesy of an honest debate.

If the NRA attempts to challenge your assertions, we are ignored. And if we try to buy advertising time or space to answer your charges, more often than not we are denied. How's that for First Amendment freedom?

Misuse of Freedom of the Press

Clearly, too many have used freedom of the press as a weapon not only to strangle our free speech, but to erode and ultimately destroy the right to keep and bear arms as well. In doing so you promoted your profession to that of constitutional judge and jury, more powerful even than our Supreme Court, more prejudiced than the Inquisition's tribunals. It is a frightening misuse of constitutional privilege, and I pray that you will come to your senses and see that these abuses are curbed.

As a veteran of World War II, as a freedom marcher who stood with Dr. Martin Luther King long before it was fashionable, and as a grandfather who wants the coming century to be free and full of promise for my grandchildren, I am . . . troubled.

The right to keep and bear arms is threatened by political theatrics, piecemeal lawmaking, talk show psychology, extreme bad taste in the entertainment industry, an ever-widening educational chasm in our schools and a conniving media, that all add up to cultural warfare against the idea that guns ever had, or should now have, an honorable and proud place in our society.

My Commitment and Vision

But all of our rights must be delivered into the 21st century as pure and complete as they came to us at the beginning of this century. Traditionally the passing of that torch is from a gnarled old hand down to an eager young one. So now, at 72, I offer my gnarled old hand.

I have accepted a call from the National Rifle Association of America to help protect the Second Amendment. I feel it is my duty to do that. My mission and vision can be summarized in three simple parts.

First, before we enter the next [twenty-first] century, I expect to see a pro-Second Amendment president in the White House.

Secondly, I expect to build an NRA with the political muscle and clout to keep a pro-Second Amendment Congress in place.

Third, is a promise to the next generation of free Americans. I hope to help raise a hundred million dollars for NRA programs and education before the year 2000. At least half of that sum will go to teach American kids what the right to keep and bear arms really means to their culture and country.

The Next Generation

We have raised a generation of young people who think that the Bill of Rights comes with their cable TV. Leave them to their channel surfing and they'll remain oblivious to history and heritage that truly matter.

Think about it—what else must young Americans think when the White House proclaims, as it did, that "a firearm in the hands of youth is a crime or an accident waiting to happen"? No—it is time they learned that firearm ownership is constitutional, not criminal. In fact, few pursuits can teach a young person more about responsibility, safety, conservation, their history and their heritage, all at once.

It is time they found out that the politically correct doctrine of today has misled them. And that when they reach legal age, if they do not break our laws, they have a right to choose to own a gun—a handgun, a long gun, a small gun, a large gun, a black gun, a purple gun, a pretty gun, an ugly gun—and to use that gun to defend themselves and their loved ones or to engage in any lawful purpose they desire without apology or explanation to anyone, ever.

This is their first freedom. If you say it's outdated, then you haven't read your own headlines. If you say guns create only carnage, I would answer that you know better. Declining morals, disintegrating families, vacillating political leadership, an eroding criminal justice system and social mores that blur right and wrong are more to blame—certainly more than any legally owned firearm.

I want to rescue the Second Amendment from an opportunistic president, and from a press that apparently can't comprehend that attacks on the Second Amendment set the stage for assaults on the First.

Saving the Second Amendment

I want to save the Second Amendment from all these nitpicking little wars of attrition—fights over alleged Saturday night specials, plastic guns, cop killer bullets and so many other made-for-prime-time non-issues invented by some press agent over at gun control headquarters that you guys buy time and again.

I simply cannot stand by and watch a right guaranteed by the Constitution of the United States come under attack from those who either can't understand it, don't like the sound of it, or find themselves too philosophically squeamish to see why it remains the first among equals: Because it is the right we turn to when all else fails.

That's why the Second Amendment is America's first freedom.

Please, go forth and tell the truth. There can be no free speech, no freedom of the press, no freedom to protest, no freedom to worship your god, no freedom to speak your mind, no freedom from fear, no freedom for your children and for theirs, for anybody, anywhere, without the Second Amendment freedom to fight for it.

If you don't believe me, just turn on the news tonight. Civilization's veneer is wearing thinner all the time.

Thank you.

Second Amendment Rights Should Be Limited

David L. Goldberg

David L. Goldberg is an assistant state's attorney in Baltimore City, Maryland. In the following selection Goldberg notes that the Supreme Court has been willing to restrict the Fourth Amendment's protections against police searches to ensure public safety. He would like to see this logic applied to the Second Amendment instead. Whether the amendment protects the state's or the individual's rights, Goldberg believes, the amendment is still limited to proper militia weapons. That means handguns, revolvers, and other small arms are simply not protected and can therefore be restricted or banned.

Because of the adolescent handgun violence in our country's schools and the shooting rampages that have struck our business districts, there have been many debates concerning the second amendment and its place in modern society. Congress has called for stricter gun-show regulations, gun locks, and a possible rise in the legal age for handgun ownership. What I do not understand is how the United States Supreme Court purports to protect us from gun violence by scaling back the fourth amendment while allowing the second amendment to go unscathed when, in fact, if a second amendment case is brought before the Court, it should be clear that no constitutional right to own a handgun exists. Let me explain.

Over the past three years the Supreme Court has handed down decisions that, in the name of public safety, have withered the once formidable fourth amendment to the Constitution. My favorite example is the Court's treatment of the

David L. Goldberg, "A Well-Regulated Militia or a Volatile Militancy?" *Criminal Justice Ethics,* vol. 19, Winter–Spring 2000, p. 2. Copyright © 2000 by The Institute for Criminal Justice Ethics, 555 W. Fifty-seventh St., Suite 601, New York, NY, 10019-1029. Reproduced by permission.

automobile. Currently, for safety in an age replete with handguns and explosives, you can be pulled over by a police officer
based upon pretext if you abruptly drive away from a stop
sign, your passenger can be ordered out of the car even though
you allegedly committed the offense, and that passenger's lug-
gage can be searched merely because such baggage is capable
of concealing contraband. I accept the argument that, due to
the pervading problems of gun violence, protection is needed.
I think the way to ensure safety, however, is not to undermine
our security against unreasonable searches and instead go to
the root of the problem—firearms. Why is it then that the
Supreme Court erodes the fourth amendment but does not
strike at the second amendment?

Interpreting the Second Amendment

Now, before everyone screams, recognize that I am not suggesting that we repeal part of the Bill of Rights. What I am
suggesting is that, like the fourth amendment recently, the
second amendment is interpretable in a manner that will
produce a safer society. The standard debate regarding the
rights afforded under the second amendment concerns whose
right it is to maintain arms under the Constitution. Scholars
have spent years arguing over whether the amendment provides a right to the states themselves or to us as individuals.
The "state's rights" advocates argue that the right to keep
and bear arms rests with the states in order to establish and
maintain militias to protect against federal tyranny. The "individual rights" school retorts that the amendment protects
an inherent individual right to protection of the home and
against any governmental oppression. Although this is the
debate that consistently arises concerning the second amendment, it is of no import under the interpretation I offer.

Regardless of whether the right lies with the state or the
individual, revolvers, automatic handguns, and numerous
small arms are not provided for under the amendment. The
second amendment reads: "A well regulated Militia, being necessary to the security of a free State, the right of the people to
keep and bear Arms, shall not be infringed." So what are
"Arms"? Did not the framers of the Constitution see the right

to bear arms as a means to check tyranny, rather than as a license to carry a handgun on the streets and so jeopardize safety?

Connection to Militias

When James Madison, with Thomas Jefferson's aid, framed the Bill of Rights, he specifically noted how the right to bear arms is integral for a regulated militia to maintain the security of a free country. Hence, the second amendment was produced to protect the citizenry against a tyrannical and oppressive government. How does a Glock-17 handgun do such a thing? Why are all these ridiculous handheld guns being sold? Please do not insult my intelligence by suggesting that they could be used for modern warfare if the government becomes despotic.

The Supreme Court's only real treatment of such discourse was in 1939, in *United States v. Miller.* In Miller, the Court noted that a shotgun having a barrel of less than eighteen inches did not have "some reasonable relationship to the preservation or efficiency of a well regulated militia." Thus, the Supreme Court itself has held that the second amendment does not guarantee the right to bear all arms because some are not military equipment. This means that there is no constitutional right to own a handgun; states should just make handgun possession illegal! Now, am I suggesting that citizens should not have the right to bear arms under eighteen inches in length (specifically handguns), but still the right to own rifles and machine guns? Maybe.

Handguns for Rifles

For safety reasons, it would arguably be better policy to deny a right to handguns and small arms because they are capable of concealment and have no true nexus to warfare in case of the need for a militia. It is more difficult for a person to sell drugs or rob a store with a gun that has a 20-inch barrel than with one that can fit in a pocket (do not think even for a minute that one can ultimately do more damage with one than with the other—all guns can kill). If the Supreme Court is really bent on protecting police officers and citizens—make those who are going to carry guns try to get away with carrying rifles on the street. They will be noticed and arrested before they even get to a corner. Law enforcement officers should be the only ones with access to small firearms so they can efficiently carry protection and enforce the law. If there is no guaranteed right to own a handgun, then a state can make it a crime to do so.

Will this cause rifle shootouts and more death? Not likely. We already have guns all over the streets, children massacring children, and handgun executions in robbery attempts. If the Supreme Court is going to limit rights, it should stay away from the fourth amendment and think more about the second. Until then, drive very carefully and do not forget your bulletproof vest.

Handguns Should Be Eliminated from Society

Josh Sugarmann

Josh Sugarmann is the executive director of the Violence Policy Center, a gun control advocacy organization. He is also the author of *NRA: Money, Firepower, and Fear.* In the following excerpt he calls for a ban on handguns because they cause most of the many homicides and suicides associated with gun violence. In doing so, he discusses the increasing deadliness of handguns and the apparent indifference of the handgun industry to the terrible human cost of its products. Overall, he finds that the costs of legal handgun ownership far outweigh the benefits. He also criticizes the gun control movement for advocating halfway measures, such as background checks and mandatory trigger locks. For Sugarmann, the only effective option is an outright ban, which he believes an increasing number of Americans are ready to accept.

The United States does not have a gun problem—it has a *handgun* problem. Our nation leads the industrialized world in firearms violence of all types because most of our violence involves handguns, which are relatively inexpensive, easy to acquire, and therefore ubiquitous.

The call to ban handguns is not inspired by a hatred of guns. It is a response to the very real blood price that our nation has paid for the explosive growth of our handgun population over the past generation. More than two out of three of the one million Americans who have died by firearms violence since 1962 were killed with handguns—a tally now in excess of 670,000. This weapon, which has inflicted pain and death in such a disproportionate degree, is owned by a small minority of Americans—surprisingly only one out of six adults. And most American guns aren't handguns. America's gun arsenal stands at more than 190 million. Two thirds are rifles and shotguns. Only one third are handguns. Despite this minority position, handguns perform their deadly role in the great majority of homicides and suicides, as well as showing up almost nine times out of 10 in nonfatal crimes—such as robbery, assault, and rape—in which guns are used.

Sixty-Five Million Handguns

The unmistakable impact of a handgun population of 65 million on our murder rate can be clearly seen by comparing ourselves to countries that severely limit access to handguns. For example, in 1995 the U.S. firearms death rate was 13.7 per 100,000; in Canada 3.9 per 100,000; in Australia 2.9 per 100,000; and in England and Wales it was 0.4 per 100,000. The main difference between those nations and our own is the difference in *lethal* violence stemming from our easy access to handguns. As public health researcher Susan P. Baker noted more than 15 years ago:

> We often hear that "Guns don't kill people, people kill people." . . . Sometimes, no doubt, a person who is intent upon killing someone seeks out a lethal weapon. Far more often, gun-inflicted deaths ensue from impromptu arguments and fights. . . . These deaths would largely be replaced by non-fatal injuries if a gun were not handy. Thus, a far more appropriate generality would be that "People without guns *injure* people; guns *kill* them."

Deadly Innovations

The modern handgun has been honed for decades by the firearms industry to achieve the highest possible level of lethality, just as race cars are continually developed for maximum speed. The rapid evolution of the handgun into a killing machine without peer is the result of a strategy developed by the gun industry to boost sales. Just as more horsepower sells cars and faster processors sell PCs, the industry has boosted sales through an increase in firepower.

What deadly innovations will the industry come up with next? We already have an idea: integral laser sights that offer the user point-and-shoot killing capability; an increase in the use of plastics to decrease weight and price, while offering eye-catching aesthetics; next-generation ammunition that promises the user devastating wound ballistics; and as always, the guiding principle of modern handgun design—the greatest lethality available in the smallest possible package.

Whether from moral blindness or the infinite human capacity for ignoring unpleasant realities, the gun industry appears totally unconcerned about the damage its products generate. As the debate over gun violence is almost always framed in terms of fatalities, it should be remembered that for every person killed with a firearm, nearly three others require medical treatment for nonfatal wounds. One conservative estimate places the annual cost of immediate medical care for all gunshot wounds at four billion dollars. Other researchers take into account lifetime care and long-term economic loss and place the overall cost of gun violence in excess of $20 billion a year. As pistols and revolvers indisputably account for the greater portion of gun deaths and injuries, handguns without doubt also impose the greatest cost. The gun industry blithely passes this bill on to the rest of us. . . .

Costs Versus Benefits

Even a rough comparison between the detrimental effects of civilian handgun ownership versus the benefits these weapons are purported to deliver yields a self-evident case for banning handguns. For every time in 1997 that a civilian used a handgun to kill in self-defense, *109* people lost their lives in handgun homicides, suicides, and unintentional death.

Recognizing these facts as their Achilles' heel, the National Rifle Association and other members of the gun lobby have disseminated wildly inflated numbers supposedly showing handguns to be an effective form of self-defense. . . . Their methodologies are dubious, and their numbers evaporate under scrutiny.

The full consequences of handgun ownership are reflected in the fact that more gun deaths are suicides rather than homicides. Obviously, firearms of themselves do not make people suicidal. But, as their numbers have grown over the years, their availability at moments of emotional crisis has also increased, an availability that all but guarantees that a suicide attempt will end in a fatality. . . .

The Hard Choice

There is effectively no handgun control in America today. Pistols and revolvers are cheap, plentiful, and available to almost anyone who wants one. The result is a level of lethal violence unmatched in the industrialized world.

The most common "solutions" offered by gun-control advocates will do nothing to change this. The disconnect between the real-life horror of handguns in America and the pale responses offered by those vested with advancing gun control is apparent to even the most casual observer. After each massacre or high-profile shooting, gun-control advocates, yoked by their own semantic noose, look to find a specific, discrete, *politically feasible* measure to advocate. The answer to the Jonesboro school massacre of children by children: trigger locks. The answer to the Columbine massacre: background checks at gun shows, and other minor tweaks to federal policy. This now predictable pattern is not only disheartening but, most important, its obvious limitations reinforce the NRA myth (and a creeping suspicion among the American public) that gun control can do nothing to stop gun violence.

Movement at a Crossroads

The gun-control movement is at a crossroads. It can either continue down a course defined by polling, politics, and the lowest common denominator—the "common sense" approach embodied in "gun safety." Or it can adopt an agenda shaped by the reality of gun violence in America that truly represents the public interest: banning handguns. Handguns *can* be banned. The only question is whether those who want to reduce gun death and injury in America—elected officials, gun-control advocates, and concerned citizens—are willing to endorse solutions that will work, not just slogans that will sell.

So what's stopping a movement to ban handguns? Not the Second Amendment: no gun-control law has *ever* been overturned by the U.S. Supreme Court on Second Amendment grounds. Federal bans on machine guns and some assault weapons, as well as city ordinances banning handgun possession, have remained on the books for decades despite vigorous court challenges. Not the facts. The unique role of the handgun in contributing to America's culture of lethal violence is well documented. Not public opinion or the views of the key institutions of our society: millions of Americans today live under a handgun ban and tens of millions are willing to. Numerous national organizations support a ban, including the American Academy of Pediatrics, American Association of Suicidology, American Jewish Congress, American Psychiatric Association, American Public Health Association, Child Welfare League of America, National Association of Social Workers, National Urban League, Presbyterian Church (USA), and the United States Conference of Mayors.

Shrinking Gun Ownership

The greatest ally of a handgun ban may be time. Gun ownership in America is shrinking. Hunting, the traditional means by which most Americans were introduced to gun ownership, is fading away. It is estimated that by the year 2020, hunting as we know it today will no longer exist. Compulsory military service, another means by which American males were historically introduced to firearms, no longer exists. Industry efforts begun in the mid-1980s to create a new handgun market by targeting America's women have failed. Having already "lost a generation" of young shooters, the industry and its gun-lobby supporters have now targeted America's youth. Yet the happy memories of aging gun owners have little relevance or interest to 21st-century youth who view the issue of "guns and kids" far differently than do their gun-loving elders.

Our nation will eventually ban handguns. The only question is whether America's gun-control movement will lead the battle, or watch it from the sidelines.

Banning Handguns Is Not a Practical Option

James B. Jacobs

James B. Jacobs is a professor of law at New York University and the author of books on drunk driving and hate crime laws. In the following excerpt from his book *Can Gun Control Work?*, he takes the position that banning handguns is impractical. After describing the history of failed attempts to limit guns in the United States, Jacobs discusses the feasibility of a ban. Comparing a gun ban to alcohol prohibition and the modern drug war, he contends that clandestine gun manufacturers would spring up to supply an active black market in illegal handguns. In addition, he suggests that lax enforcement and lenient prosecution would undercut the effort to keep guns out of the hands of otherwise law-abiding citizens. These factors, combined with serious constitutional issues, make prohibition of handguns little more than a hopeful slogan in Jacobs's opinion.

In the United States, proposals for universal handgun prohibition are relatively recent, although most of the western states in the mid-nineteenth century had laws against *carrying* concealed weapons. Efforts to prevent people from owning or possessing firearms altogether first arose in the Black Codes passed by the southern states after the Civil War. The former Confederate states passed laws to prevent former slaves from exercising any rights, especially the right to own firearms. The Civil Rights Act of 1866 and the Fourteenth Amendment were both aimed at reversing the disarmament and subjugation of the former slaves. In the latter decades of the nineteenth century and early decades of the twentieth century, some politicians advocated that aliens be denied the right to keep and bear arms. Some New Dealers favored the idea of handgun prohibition and tried unsuccessfully to have handguns covered by the 1934 NFA [National Firearms Act].

Until the 1960s, no politician or criminologist seriously urged prohibition of handguns, much less all firearms. The 1930–1931 Wickersham Commission, the first national commission on crime, did not even place "guns" or "firearms" in its index. Rather, that commission focused on the emergence of organized crime groups that trafficked alcoholic beverages and corrupted government agents. While the commission criticized law enforcement officers for "too free and easy use of firearms," it did not even mention possible options for regulating private citizens' access to guns.

President's Commission of 1967

The 1967 President's Commission on Law Enforcement and the Administration of Justice assigned a task force to gun violence. That task force concluded that federal firearms regulation, particularly the 1938 Federal Firearms Act, had "an extremely limited effect." It found that only eight states required firearms permits, although some counties and cities had more restrictive gun controls. Nevertheless, would-be purchasers in restrictive jurisdictions could easily obtain a gun by traveling to a permissive jurisdiction to make a purchase.

The President's Commission recommended outlawing "military-type firearms" (bazookas, machine guns, and other "military-type" devices); prohibiting certain categories of dangerous individuals from possessing any firearms ("habitual drunkards, drug addicts, mental incompetents, persons with a history of mental disturbance, and persons convicted of certain offenses"); creating a federal registration system for rifles, shotguns, and handguns; requiring persons to obtain permits to possess or carry handguns: banning mail-order sales of handguns; and delaying interstate sales of rifles and shotguns to give local law enforcement officials an opportunity to block the sale.

The President's Commission criticized the NRA [National Rifle Association] for lobbying against regulations that do nothing more than "inconvenience" the legitimate gun owner. In short, the commission favored strengthening existing firearms laws, while recognizing the importance of "affording citizens ample opportunity to purchase weapons for legitimate purposes."

Until 1970, no major criminologist called for prohibiting handguns. For example, [Mittie D.] Sutherland and [Donald R.] Cressey, authors of *Principles of Criminology,* the leading criminology textbook for much of the twentieth century, only touched on firearms in a general discussion of the increasing number of deaths resulting from interaction between police and criminals. Handguns were not mentioned, although the authors criticized the "war on crime" mentality that had led to an arms race between police and civilians. They did not recommend banning or even restricting firearms availability. . . .

Congressional Prohibition Proposals

In 1973, Representative Ronald Dellums (D-Calif.) introduced the first federal handgun prohibition bill. It aimed to prevent lawless and irresponsible use of firearms by prohibiting "the importation, manufacture, sale, purchase, transfer, receipt, possession, or transportation of *handguns.*" Because the bill prohibited handgun *possession,* all handgun owners would have to give up their arms or face the consequences. . . .

In June 1992, Senators John Chafee (R-R.I.), Claiborne Pell (D-R.I.), and Alan Cranston (D-Calif.) introduced legislation to ban the sale, manufacture, and possession of handguns, with exceptions for law enforcement personnel and licensed target clubs. Senator Chafee exhorted his colleagues: "It is time to act. We cannot go on like this. Ban them!" The bill did not provide compensation to those who surrendered their handguns.

In 1993, Representative Major Robert Owens (D-N.Y.) proposed that it be "unlawful for a person to manufacture, import, export, sell, buy, transfer, receive, own, possess, transport, or use a handgun or handgun ammunition." He exempted military

personnel, registered security service guards, and licensed
handgun clubs and their members. In addition, licensed manufacturers, importers, and dealers "as necessary" were exempted
in order to satisfy the limited remaining market. The bill proposed to reimburse gun owners, who voluntarily surrendered
their firearms to a law enforcement agency within 180 days. Vi-
olators would face a maximum fine of $5,000 and five years im-
prisonment. . . .

The Feasibility of Prohibition

Prohibition proposals come in different styles and sizes. Prohibiting manufacture of handguns would be the easiest form
of prohibition to implement and enforce. The Census of Manufacturers for 1997 shows that there were one hundred and
ninety-one small arms manufacturing companies with combined sales of $1.2 billion. The locations of these manufactur-
ers are known. The federal government could order them shut
down, subject them to prohibitive taxation ("tax them to
death"), or expose them to ruinous tort liability. Their decom-
mission would be easy to monitor. Of course, the government
would need to permit at least one private company to continue
producing enough handguns for the police and whatever other
groups would still be lawfully armed. Alternatively, the government could set up its own handgun manufacturing plant
to supply the legitimate market.

Closing down legitimate manufacturers would be a boon
to black market producers. Clandestine handgun manufacturers would spring up, just as thousands of illegal stills op-
erated during alcohol prohibition, and hundreds or
thousands of clandestine labs now produce unlawful mood
and mind-altering drugs like amphetamine and ecstasy.
Even today, "zip guns" are produced or assembled in small
workshops within the United States. These black market
manufacturers, already illegal, operate outside any regulatory scheme for recordkeeping, serial numbers, safety locks,
or taxation.

Implementing a prohibition on *importation* of handguns
would be even more difficult. Without (or with sharply di-
minished) domestic U.S. sources for new handguns, there

would be a greater economic incentive for smugglers to bring in handguns from abroad. Is there any reason to believe that customs officials and other law enforcement personnel would be more successful in preventing handgun smuggling than in preventing drug smuggling? I think not. Contraband handguns, like illicit drugs, would enter the country illegally in seaborne containers, trucks, cars, planes, and by mail. (Currently, there are firearms black markets in Western Europe, where handguns smuggled from Eastern Europe and the former Soviet Union are easily obtainable in Amsterdam, Brussels, and other cities.) . . .

Enforcement Problems

Who would enforce handgun disarmament and with what degree of vigor? National Alcohol Prohibition was enforced by a small number of U.S. Treasury Department agents and by state and local police departments. Criminal justice and organized crime scholar Humbert S. Nelli writes that "Prohibition overburdened the criminal justice system and undermined respect for the nation's law." . . . In many cities, the police were contemptuous of alcohol prohibition and did not enforce it; corruption flourished. History has repeated itself with the contemporary drug war. . . .

Some prosecutors, for political or practical reasons, would hesitate to prosecute unlawful possession cases, just as prosecutors today do not prosecute every drug possession case. They would face serious difficulties convicting defendants with no criminal record who claim to possess a gun for self-defense or sport. Currently, federal prosecutors decline to prosecute a high percentage of charges even against persons *with felony records* when, though possessing firearms illegally, the arrested person has committed no other crime. It would be much more difficult to convince federal or state prosecutors to bring charges against otherwise law-abiding persons for merely violating National Handgun Prohibition. Even if prosecutors brought charges, it would be difficult to get unanimous guilty verdicts from jurors who, in many states, would be inclined to nullify the unpopular law.

Perhaps enforcing unpopular, or at least controversial, handgun disarmament could be made easier by setting the punishment low. If illegal possession of a handgun were treated as a misdemeanor or administrative violation, punishable by a small fine, say $250 or $500, jury trials could be avoided altogether. However, under that scheme, people who were committed to keeping their handguns would be no more deterred from violating the gun law than from violating the speed limit.

Coping with the Black Market

National Handgun Prohibition, whether actively or passively enforced, would have to contend with a black market. If the lawful supply of firearms was shut down, consider how easily guns could migrate into the black market. In the United States, there exists a black market in handguns that are stolen, purchased for unlawful sale, or otherwise diverted from lawful owners to criminals. According to Gary Kleck, "There appears to be stronger evidence pointing to theft as a major source of guns for criminals than illicit trafficking." Perhaps half of the guns obtained by criminals have been stolen at some time in the past, though not necessarily by the criminal who most recently possessed it and used it in a crime. Kleck estimates that as many as 750,000 guns are stolen each year. Of the inmates interviewed by sociologists James Wright and Peter Rossi in 1986, thirty-two percent said that they stole their most recently acquired handgun; 46% stated that their most recently acquired handgun was "definitely stolen," while another 24% said the gun was "probably stolen." Even in countries with strong prohibitory regimes (like Japan and Holland), criminals are able to obtain handguns relatively easily on the black market.

We can reasonably estimate that there would be a stock of some 100 million or more handguns in private hands by the time National Handgun Prohibition was enacted (assuming booming sales in the 4–5 years leading up to prohibition). The handgun black market would be supplied by imports, stolen handguns, handguns illegally produced in clandestine workshops, and handguns given away or sold by lawful owners, who oppose the law or who, for a profit, are willing to risk getting caught. . . .

The Constitutionality of Handgun Prohibition

National Handgun Prohibition would face intense constitutional attack. During the several years that it would take for the issue to reach the Supreme Court, there would be numerous federal district court decisions. If, as seems likely, some of these lower federal courts struck down handgun prohibition as unconstitutional, it would create an unsettled and ambiguous legal environment, strengthening the resolve of gun rights advocates. It would also trigger an extraordinary demand for handguns in those jurisdictions where they could still be legally purchased.

If the Supreme Court struck down National Handgun Prohibition as violative of the Second Amendment, the only other possible strategy for prohibitionists would be repeal of the Second Amendment by a constitutional amendment. Because of the super-majority required to amend the Constitution (three-quarters of the states), this would be even harder to accomplish politically than federal handgun prohibition itself. If the Supreme Court upheld the constitutionality of a National Handgun Prohibition, the disarmament law would be valid, but difficult issues of implementation, enforcement, and punishment would have to be faced.

The Devil Is in the Details

"Prohibition" is a slogan. What it means and how it would be implemented and enforced are questions that have hardly begun to be addressed. The devil is in the details. What groups and individuals would be exempted from the prohibition? Would all firearms be prohibited or just handguns? National Handgun Prohibition could apply to manufacture, importation, sale, or possession. Ending manufacture of new guns would be easiest to implement, but more than 100 million handguns would by then be in private hands, augmented by imports and the production of small clandestine shops. Prohibiting possession would require disarming the citizenry; whether done quickly or over a long period, it would be a monumental challenge, fraught with danger. Millions of citizens would not surrender their handguns. If black market activity in connection with the drug laws is any indication, a decades-long "war on handguns" might resemble a low-grade civil war more than a law enforcement initiative.

The Origins of the American Bill of Rights

The U.S. Constitution as it was originally created and submitted to the colonies for ratification in 1787 did not include what we now call the Bill of Rights. This omission was the cause of much controversy as Americans debated whether to accept the new Constitution and the new federal government it created. One of the main concerns voiced by opponents of the document was that it lacked a detailed listing of guarantees of certain fundamental individual rights. These critics did not succeed in preventing the Constitution's ratification, but were in large part responsible for the existence of the Bill of Rights.

In 1787 the United States consisted of thirteen former British colonies that had been loosely bound since 1781 by the Articles of Confederation. Since declaring their independence from Great Britain in 1776, the former colonies had established their own colonial governments and constitutions, eight of which had bills of rights written into them. One of the most influential was Virginia's Declaration of Rights. Drafted largely by planter and legislator George Mason in 1776, the seventeen-point document combined philosophical declarations of natural rights with specific limitations on the powers of government. It served as a model for other state constitutions.

The sources for these declarations of rights included English law traditions dating back to the 1215 Magna Carta and the 1689 English Bill of Rights—two historic documents that provided specific legal guarantees of the "true, ancient, and indubitable rights and liberties of the people" of England. Other legal sources included the colonies' original charters, which declared that colonists should have the same "privileges, franchises, and immunities" that they would if they lived in England. The ideas concerning natural rights developed by John Locke and other English philosophers were also influential. Some of these concepts of rights had been cited in the Declaration of Independence to justify the American Revolution.

Unlike the state constitutions, the Articles of Confederation, which served as the national constitution from 1781 to 1788, lacked a bill of rights. Because the national government under the Articles of Confederation had little authority by design, most people believed it posed little threat to civil liberties, rendering a bill of rights unnecessary. However, many influential leaders criticized the very weakness of the national government for creating its own problems; it did not create an effective system for conducting a coherent foreign policy, settling disputes between states, printing money, and coping with internal unrest.

It was against this backdrop that American political leaders convened in Philadelphia in May 1787 with the stated intent to amend the Articles of Confederation. Four months later the Philadelphia Convention, going beyond its original mandate, created a whole new Constitution with a stronger national government. But while the new Constitution included a few provisions protecting certain civil liberties, it did not include any language similar to Virginia's Declaration of Rights. Mason, one of the delegates in Philadelphia, refused to sign the document. He listed his objections in an essay that began:

> There is no Declaration of Rights, and the Laws of the general government being paramount to the laws and constitution of the several States, the Declaration of Rights in the separate States are no security.

Mason's essay was one of hundreds of pamphlets and other writings produced as the colonists debated whether to ratify the new Constitution (nine of the thirteen colonies had to officially ratify the Constitution for it to go into effect). The supporters of the newly drafted Constitution became known as Federalists, while the loosely organized group of opponents were called Antifederalists. Antifederalists opposed the new Constitution for several reasons. They believed the presidency would create a monarchy, Congress would not be truly representative of the people, and state governments would be endangered. However, the argument that proved most effective was that the new document lacked a bill of rights and thereby threatened Americans with the loss of cherished individual liberties. Federalists realized that to gain the support of key states such as New York and Virginia, they needed to pledge to offer amendments to the Constitution that would be added immediately after its ratification. Indeed, it was not until this promise was made that the requisite number of colonies ratified the document. Massachusetts, Virginia, South Carolina, New Hampshire, and New York all included amendment recommendations as part of their decisions to ratify.

One of the leading Federalists, James Madison of Virginia, who was elected to the first Congress to convene under the new Constitution, took the lead in drafting the promised amendments. Under the process provided for in the Constitution, amendments needed to be passed by both the Senate and House of Representatives and then ratified by three-fourths of the states. Madison sifted through the suggestions provided by the states and drew upon the Virginia Declaration of Rights and other state documents in composing twelve amendments, which he introduced to Congress in September 1789. "If they are incorporated into the constitution," he argued in a speech introducing his proposed amendments,

> Independent tribunals of justice will consider themselves in a peculiar manner the guardians of those rights; they will be an impenetrable bulwark against every assumption of power in the legislative or executive; they will be naturally led to resist every encroachment upon rights expressly stipulated for in the constitution by the declaration of rights.

After debate and some changes to Madison's original proposals, Congress approved the twelve amendments and sent them to the states for ratification. Two amendments were not ratified; the remaining ten became known as the Bill of Rights. Their ratification by the states was completed on December 15, 1791.

Supreme Court Cases Involving the Right to Bear Arms

1875

United States. v. Cruikshank
The Court ruled that the Second Amendment forbids only Congress, not the states, from infringing on the right of the people to bear arms.

1886

Presser v. Illinois
The Court ruled that the Second Amendment does not prevent state legislatures from regulating guns; however, because the entire nation has an interest in the reserve militia, states cannot completely "prohibit the people from keeping and bearing arms."

1894

Miller v. Texas
The Court found that Texas has the right to pass a law against carrying weapons. However, the Court specifically rejected the defendant's claim that the Fourteenth Amendment "incorporated" the Second Amendment into state law.

1939

United States v. Miller
The Court declared that the federal government is permitted to regulate or ban firearms that have no obvious relationship to maintaining a well-regulated militia. At the same time, the Court noted that militia members, if called up, were expected to report for duty with their own weapons, implying a fundamental right to private gun ownership of some kind.

1968

Burton v. Sills
The Court dismissed the claims of gun dealers and sportsmen that a strict New Jersey gun control law violated their rights, finding no substantial federal violation.

1980

Lewis v. United States
The Court ruled that the federal government has the right to prevent felons from owning guns.

1990

United States v. Verdugo-Urquidez
In a case that centered on the Fourth Amendment rights of nonresident aliens in a foreign country, the Court noted that "the people" seems to have a similar meaning in the First, Second, Fourth, and other amendments. While some see this ruling as an affirmation that the right to bear arms is an individual right, like the right to free speech, others note that this particular ruling does not address the militia clause that is central to arguments about the Second Amendment.

1994

Staples v. United States
The Court found that the government, in order to win conviction under a federal gun control law, must prove that a defendant knowingly possesses a banned firearm.

1995

United States v. Lopez
The Court struck down the federal Gun-Free School Zones Act, finding that Congress had overstretched its power to regulate interstate commerce in applying it to guns in schools.

1997

Printz v. United States
The Court declared that the background check provision of the Brady Handgun Violence Prevention Act unfairly burdens

local law enforcement. Since then, the FBI has instituted a national database for instant background checks.

2002

Appeal of United States v. Emerson (2001)
In this instance, the Supreme Court spoke by rejecting an appeal. The Fifth U.S. Circuit Court of Appeals upheld the conviction of a man for violating a federal law banning gun ownership by those under a restraining order. At the same time, it noted that the Second Amendment protects "individual rights," which could only be limited in specific instances. By appealing the decision, Attorney General John Ashcroft hoped to get the Supreme Court to declare itself in favor of the Fifth Circuit's interpretation, but the Supreme Court declined to hear the case.

Books

Les Adams, *The Second Amendment Primer: A Citizen's Guidebook to the History, Sources, and Authorities for the Constitutional Guarantee of the Right to Keep and Bear Arms.* Richmond, IN: Palladium, 1996.

Marjolijn Bijlefeld, *The Gun Control Debate: A Documentary History.* Westport, CT: Greenwood, 1997.

Carl T. Bogus, ed., *The Second Amendment in Law and History: Historians and Constitutional Scholars on the Right to Bear Arms.* New York: New Press, 2000.

Peter H. Brown and Daniel G. Abel, *Outgunned: Up Against the NRA: The First Complete Insider Account of the Battle over Gun Control.* New York: Free Press, 2003.

Saul Cornell et al., *Whose Right to Bear Arms Did the Second Amendment Protect?* New York: St. Martin's, 2000.

Robert J. Cottrol, *Gun Control and the Constitution: Sources and Explorations on the Second Amendment.* New York: Garland, 1993.

Clayton E. Cramer, *For the Defense of Themselves and the State: The Original Intent and Judicial Interpretation of the Right to Keep and Bear Arms.* Westport, CT: Praeger, 1994.

Osha Gray Davidson, *Under Fire: The NRA and the Battle for Gun Control.* Iowa City: University of Iowa Press, 1998.

Stephen P. Halbrook, *That Every Man Be Armed: The Evolution of a Constitutional Right.* Albuquerque: University of New Mexico Press, 1984.

Dennis A. Henigan, E. Bruce Nicholson, and David Hemenway, *Guns and the Constitution: The Myth of Second Amendment Protection for Firearms in America.* Northampton, MA: Aletheia, 1995.

James B. Jacobs, *Can Gun Control Work?* New York: Oxford University Press, 2002.

David B. Kopel, *The Samurai, the Mountie, and the Cowboy: Should America Adopt the Gun Controls of Other Democracies?* Amherst, NY: Prometheus, 1992.

Wayne LaPierre, *Guns, Crime, and Freedom.* Washington, DC: Regnery, 1994.

———, *Guns, Freedom, and Terrorism.* Nashville, TN: WND, 2003.

John R. Lott Jr., *The Bias Against Guns: Why Almost Everything You've Heard About Gun Control Is Wrong.* Washington, DC: Regnery, 2003.

———, *More Guns, Less Crime: Understanding Crime and Gun-Control Laws.* Chicago: University of Chicago Press, 1998.

Joyce Lee Malcolm, *To Keep and Bear Arms: The Origins of an Anglo-American Right.* Cambridge, MA: Harvard University Press, 1994.

Andrew J. McClurg, David B. Kopel, and Brannon P. Denning, eds., *Gun Control and Gun Rights: A Reader and Guide.* New York: New York University Press, 2000.

Robert J. Spitzer, *The Politics of Gun Control.* Washington, DC: CQ Press, 2004.

Josh Sugarmann, *Every Handgun Is Aimed at You: The Case for Banning Handguns.* New York: New Press, 2001.

William J. Vizzard, *Shots in the Dark: The Policy, Politics, and Symbolism of Gun Control.* Lanham, MD: Rowman & Littlefield, 2000.

William Weir, *A Well-Regulated Militia: The Battle over Gun Control.* North Haven, CT: Archon, 1997.

David E. Young, *The Origin of the Second Amendment: A Documentary History of the Bill of Rights in Commentaries on Liberty, Free Government and an Armed Populace, 1787–1792.* Ontanagan, MI: Golden Oak, 1995.

Franklin E. Zimring and Gordon Hawkins, *The Citizen's Guide to Gun Control.* New York: Macmillan, 1987.

Web Sites

Brady Center to Prevent Gun Violence, www.bradycenter. org. Headed by Sarah Brady, whose husband, James Brady, was shot during the attempted assassination of President Ronald Reagan, this organization's Web site provides numerous resources, including lists of court cases and links to articles emphasizing the Second Amendment's purpose in maintaining a "well-regulated militia."

The Coalition to Stop Gun Violence: New to the Issue, www.csgv.org/new. An organization devoted to gun control, CSGV also provides basic information on Supreme Court opinions and other materials that favor the "collective rights" interpretation of the Second Amendment.

FindLaw Constitution Center, www.findlaw.com/casecode/ constitution. A clearinghouse for lawyers, law students, and the public, this site provides links to case law and judicial interpretation of the Constitution and its amendments, including the Second Amendment.

National Rifle Association/Institute for Legislative Action, www.nraila.org. The political arm of the nation's largest gun ownership organization provides information on federal and state legislation related to gun control and makes the case for Second Amendment protection of individual gun rights.

Second Amendment Foundation, www.saf.org. The Web site of this organization, a strong proponent of the individual right to keep and bear arms, provides information on the Second Amendment, state constitutional protections of the right to bear arms, links to publications and debates, and numerous other resources.

INDEX